INSIDE PASSAGE

INSIDE PASSAGE

a memoir

KEEMA WATERFIELD

GREEN WRITERS PRESS | *Brattleboro, Vermont*

Printed in the United States

10 9 8 7 6 5 4 3 2 1

Green Writers Press is a Vermont-based publisher whose mission is to spread a message of hope and renewal through the words and images we publish. Throughout we will adhere to our commitment to preserving and protecting the natural resources of the earth. To that end, a percentage of our proceeds will be donated to environmental activist groups and the author's focus donation. Green Writers Press gratefully acknowledges support from individual donors, friends, and readers to help support the environment and our publishing initiative.

Giving Voice to Writers & Artists Who Will Make the World a Better Place

Green Writers Press | Brattleboro, Vermont
www.greenwriterspress.com

ISBN: 978-1950584567

Cover art by Fawn Waterfield.

THE PAPER USED IN THIS PUBLICATION IS PRODUCED BY MILLS COMMITTED
TO RESPONSIBLE AND SUSTAINABLE FORESTRY PRACTICES.

For my mother, my first love story.
And my children, the sequel.

~

I would like to begin by respectfully acknowledging that I live and write in the unceded territories of the Séliš (Salish or "Flathead") and Qlispé (upper Kalispel or Pend d'Oreille) Peoples. I honor their stewardship of this land and its life-giving rivers, and their continued guidance in caring for this place for generations to come.

I also respectfully acknowledge that I was born in and imprinted upon the unceded traditional land of the Dena'ina People, where much of this story takes place. It is a place of great beauty and strength, and I honor their enduring care and commitment to the land and water that has shaped me from birth.

Additionally, I respectfully acknowledge that I spent my formative years on the unceded traditional land of the Lingít (Tlingit). I honor their abiding commitment to the land and water, and their rich cultural legacy of song and dance that so deeply informed my childhood.

I make this acknowledgement out of gratitude to the Séliš, Qlispé, Denai'na, and Lingít People, and all Indigenous people who have been in relationship with this land for generations, past and present, and also in recognition of the historical and ongoing legacy of colonialism. The story I am living has unfolded at every step upon lands whose traditional occupants have and do endure terrible hardships as a cost of systemic colonialist infringements. I would like to honor the Indigenous people of this country with remembrance and a call to work together as a nation to dismantle colonial practices.

INSIDE PASSAGE

Introduction

~~~

"Looks like you're going to have that baby any minute," a guy at the table nearest the stage says. He has weekend stubble and the cargo shorts-paired-with-flip-flops thing going. It's Sunday evening at a local brewery in a mountain city in Montana, so he fits right in. "Don't worry. I got you if it goes down." He raises a full pint glass in salute. "I'm an EMT."

I smile, adjust my mic stand, and do a mental eye roll. Wouldn't that be fun? Delivering my baby on a brewhouse floor with a drunk heckler to assist?

"The baby should make it through a couple more songs," I say, strumming my guitar. "This one's a true story."

I only play music for the fun of it: a few originals, a few covers. Mostly early evening shows at breweries and distilleries, and art galleries. I thought for a time that I might make music my life's work one day, but I let college suck me in instead. Then more college, some travel, marriage, now kids. Besides, without my sister's songbird highs and my mother's silken lows, what good is my own voice to me beyond casual enjoyment?

I remain a lazy musician, wholly averse to the hustle. My sister's doing it: late-night gigs, radio appearances, an album a year, the occasional indie film score. It looks good on her. It also looks hard.

I played with my daughter strapped to my back when she was tiny, but she's recently discovered the power of her legs on an open dance floor, the thrill of fast circles in a crowd of dancers. Very little in this world feels as perfect and true as picking my way through a song with my kid out there, holding hands with her best friend, working her way through a toddler two-step until they fall on top of each other, laughing, in the small space they've carved out in the crowd. The smile in my husband's eyes as he lifts them back up and teaches them to spin each other.

Tonight's show has gone past bedtime. My daughter aims tired eyes my way at the end of a slow tune and blinks heavily. I know what's on her mind. She shakes loose from her father, makes her way to the stage, and climbs up. I set my guitar in the stand, lean into a stool, and pull her to my lap for the last song. She curls her legs under the round curve of the baby in my belly and lays her head against my heart, singing along. She knows these songs already.

As we're packing up, the EMT stops by. "Making a family band?" he asks, nodding at my daughter, busily strumming my guitar now nestled in its case.

His question summons the yaw and snap of our family tent in a Southeast Alaskan wind, my mother and siblings pressed close under our shared blankets. Ravens cawing from the trees outside, a sea of campers rousing for another day of bass and fiddle and guitar in the endless string of music festivals that may have been the happiest and loneliest part of my life. The creosote and steel tang of the harbor as we board yet another ferry, bound for Ketchikan or Juneau or Sitka or Haines, compelled by our family curse to chase the music and wander, wander, wander. The loneliness of being perpetual new kids softened by the sweetness of Mom's guitar on her lap, my siblings and I on the floor at her feet reading an endless pile of books and jumping in when the harmony grabs us. The pure knowing. *This is my place.*

"I would do that again," I say.

By Any Other

~~~

"Make sure the drunks sleep outside," my mother says, splashing cold water on her mouth at the trailer's kitchen sink. She pulls long, dark hair away from her face and leans in, drinking deeply from a cupped hand. She gasps and lays her head across one arm on the lip of the sink.

Twenty years and change, my mother is all belly and glowing olive skin and great doe eyes. Freckles form bright constellations along her cheeks and arms. Summer stardust, she calls them.

She pushes away from the sink and leans her petite frame into my father's massive one, nearly a foot taller than her. He is forty years old, broad-shouldered, and tan in a way that Nordic redheads only ever manage through repeated sunburn. His given name is David, but he's been Dude since his first set of kids were toddlers who couldn't quite manage "dad" more than ten years earlier.

She'd met Dude at a music festival and fallen in love with him on sight. Compared to the martial law of her mother's home, Dude's free spirit had seemed like a dream. She'd taken in his booming voice and broad muscles, the red curls springing from his damp forehead, chin, and chest, and told him: "I'm going to have your babies." He might have been twice her age, with two teenage kids and an ex-wife down the street, but what did that matter? She had a plan.

The screen door of the trailer slaps open, and a neighbor leans in with a small wood pipe. "Hey, Dude. Some fresh to take the edge off?" Dude accepts the pipe, gently presses the fragrant green bud with the butt of his lighter into the bowl, and tokes. Outside, someone strums a guitar and plays through a few bars before a fiddle jumps in.

"On the other end of this day, we will have the most beautiful baby in the world," my mother sighs.

Dude nods, blowing smoke. "The most beautiful," he says.

Or at least that's how I imagine it because stories vary as to whether the sun shone or clouds came right down to the ground on the late July day when my mother gave birth to me, so I've had to piece the event together over time. Sadly, most of the guests crammed into my father's doublewide trailer on Kona Lane were as befuddled as kittens, and no one can recall the exact day I emerged.

To be fair, some of the attendees were drunk as well as stoned. The party had started with the onset of contractions, which can last somewhere between ten minutes and eternity, according to anyone who's ever been in labor. It's no wonder the facts of my birth are muddled.

"I wanted you born into a community," my mother says. "Used to be children were born into homes with three and four generations under one roof, but we didn't have that in Anchorage, so I made one for you." Three or four generations in that dinky trailer is a frightening thought (*mobile home*, my mother insists). So when I think about it, I like to imagine a great big house with a parlor for the birthing and the dying and a wraparound deck for the barefoot banjo picking. But this was Anchorage, Alaska, in 1980. Wraparound decks weren't a common sight for trailers, or even normal houses, then.

Instead, my mother paced a fifteen-second loop around the bed, through the door to the toilet and back. She hummed through contractions, flashing thumbs up as friendly partygoers popped in to cheer her on with sloshing cans of Rainier beer.

I'd call that tight quarters, maybe even go so far as claustrophobic, but Mom says it was intimate. And she says it in such a way as to mean: *I'd never been happier or more in love with the world, and if a thousand people had walked through that door, it wouldn't have changed a thing.*

When I imagine that moment, I see my tiny hippie mother with her black hair falling to her butt, dark eyes wide and wondering as she breathes through her first childbirth, and she is in full bliss mode. When the pain is intense, she doubles over and says, "Goddess, help me!" When the pain is light, she sings, "*Summertime, and the living is eaaaaasy.*"

Then from the front door, I hear a raspy man's voice, "Fawn, where's that baby? Let's get this party started." I have very few major childhood memories without some pleasant drunk guy interjecting something totally ridiculous and inappropriate during a magical moment. I can't even summon an imaginary scene without *that guy* popping up.

Among the community members invited to the party-that-was-my-birth were my father's oldest children from his first (and only) marriage: Zachary and Cimberlee (as in Kimberly with a "k" but with a devil-may-care slant to the spelling). Zach and Cim were teenagers then, and as the children of a well-known Anchorage pot dealer, I doubt my birth party was their first hoedown. Also in attendance were two out of three of my future stepdads: C.A. and Brian. I can't summon a single thing to be grateful to Brian for, but I have C.A. to thank for saving my life that day when he invited a friend to the party who knew a midwife.

The way Kim remembers it, she got a call out of the blue from her friend, C.A., who was attending a birthing party. Some years before, Kim had assisted a midwife with a few births, but she had no formal training and balked at the request. "Listen," C.A. told her, "there's a twenty-year-old girl in labor right now with her first baby. It's coming with or without you, and I'm pretty sure there's not one person here who knows what to do about it." I can imagine Kim pacing her living room, debating whether to call her midwife friend. Picking up the phone. Putting it down. The worried circle of her thoughts until, finally, she got up the courage to at least *ask*.

When I eventually drew my first breath, it was thanks to Kim's midwife friend. She'd show up in time to unravel the umbilical cord wrapped three times firmly around my neck. Then she thumped me vigorously on the back until I got pissed off enough to scream about it.

By that time, according to legend, most of the partygoers had dropped like smoked-out bees, so my mother and I had us a nice long getting-to-know-you spell through the quiet hours. We laid awake all night, breathing each other in. She hummed "Summertime" and stroked my cheeks and promised to love me always. All these years later, I still can't sing that song without yawning and feeling the ghost of her hand stroking the hair back from my forehead.

"Hello, Keema," she said, nudging a finger into my clenched newborn fist. "I've been waiting to meet you for a long time." I curled into her voice, settling into the familiar comfort of it.

I must have seemed a changeling in her arms, all red fuzz and ivory skin, eyes the exact shifting blue-grey of the Wrangell Narrows. In photos, I shone like a small surprise against the backdrop of her long, dark, Black Irish hair, wide coffee-colored eyes, and coppery skin.

She may not remember the date of my birth, but she recalls our first quiet hours the way you might recollect the wonder of warm socks on the first cold day of the year.

"You came out with your eyes wide open," Mom likes to say. Except when I tell stories about our growing-up-together years. Then she rolls her eyes and says, "I should have known you'd write about it all."

~

For four-and-a-half months I had my mother to myself. Four-and-a-half months of coos and kisses, dance parties, and long wakeful nights staring into each other's eyes. There were surely tears on both our parts. And quiet moments lying side by side, inhaling each other's breath. Becoming. Four-and-a-half months in which something so strong and painfully important grew between us that I've spent the rest of my life trying to elbow my way back into the circle of her arms.

Four-and-a-half months.

Then two cells became four, became eight, sixteen, thirty-two until eventually, they blossomed into a girl just like me, but longer and hungrier and crankier. A sister filling up that womb I had only just left.

Tekla got it easy. She was named for our father's Finnish grandmother. Tekla means "pearl." The name carries history since we're third-generation Americans on our father's side. I'm still not sure whether that means his mother was born here or moved here as a girl because I never met my father's parents. Tekla got a piece of our father with her name, which maybe gave her something to hold onto through the years of radio silence.

For most of my childhood, what I knew of my father could be tallied on one hand: his name wasn't really Dude, but everyone called him that, our red hair came from him, and my sister was named after his grandmother. The rest is a question mark I've chased all my life.

It's the first thing people ask. *Keema?* they say. Or, more often: *Kina? Tina? Kim?* Then, *What an unusual name.* Or, *Is it short for something? What does it mean?* As if with my name, I've gone and volunteered some new existential crisis they have to pick apart before bedtime, or they'll never sleep again. Perfect strangers will stand by, receipt and bags in hand, to listen to the story of my name when I get carded at the grocery store, and a clerk innocently asks about it.

It was my mother's name first. In third grade, her Camp Fire class made up names for themselves, drawing on words from various Native American languages that represented their young selves (*bird watcher, artist, tree climber*). Then, in an act of imaginative play and cultural appropriation, they took the first letter from each word and lined them up to create an all-new name. Mom's letters landed on X-E-E-M-A, which struck her brain as toxic somehow, so she threw out the "X" and went hunting through the alphabet for a more romantic consonant, eventually landing on "K."

There were times I laid awake imagining who I'd be now if I had one of those other names Mom tried on. I'd run the alphabet and consider the many consonants my mother had to choose from: Deema, Feema, Geema, Heema, Jeema, Zeema. Then, for kicks, I'd imagine myself as a Mary, Kristy, or Tiffany with a high, side ponytail. An Anne, Jordan, or Tristen. Or, knowing my mother's hippie heart: Rainbow, Leaf That Sings, Sunshine, Dharma, Om.

Once they've figured out the spelling, many strangers feel compelled to share odd bits of trivia with me:

In South Asia, the traditional minced meat dish used in kebabs and naan is called keema.

One of the Buddha's original female disciples was called Khema.

There is an independent learning school in California called Keema High (Home of the Wildcats!), which is only notable in that I am a Leo who dropped out of high school.

I once heard that my name translates to "girl" in Hawaiian, while someone else said it means "faces the wind" in one of the many Alaskan Native tongues (I've never been able to verify this claim). A friend of mine from Saudi Arabia says my name sounds phonetically like the Arabic word qeema, which means "value."

In high school, I had a Vietnamese boyfriend by the name of Thang, who stood a solid twelve inches taller than me and, the way

I remember it, had the arms and shoulders of a wrestler. Whenever his mother answered the door, she tittered at the sight of me. "Thang!" she'd holler over her shoulder. "Your girlfriend's here!" Then she'd press her hand to her mouth, shoulders trembling with silent laughter as I moved on down the hall.

It went like that for months before I finally asked: "Am I missing something?"

Thang smiled and bent to kiss my cheek. "It's your name," he said. "Didn't I tell you? It's . . . uh. Well . . . dog poop. In Vietnamese, I mean."

It boils down to this: in third grade, my mother knew she would grow up to have a redheaded daughter and that she would name her Keema—this being no small miracle considering her dark eyes and hair. Thereafter she named all of her favorite dolls Keema and told everyone about the little girl she would have one day.

She had a plan, my mother. And that plan was me.

When you break it down, my name means "daughter of Fawn." Sometimes that's all the answer I give.

Dude's Gone Baby

~~~

I did it because Mom told me not to. I looked her in the eye and reached right up to the woodstove in Grandma's living room in Petersburg, Alaska, laying three chubby fingers and part of my right palm just above the little flame-licked window in the black iron door. Mom snatched me off the ground and ran to the kitchen sink in that thin, hard silence between shock and scream, already streaming cold water over my hand before I began to wail. Tekla crawled naked to the couch, pulled her feet under her, and leaned against it, covering her ears with splayed hands. She did a worried jig, red eyebrows pulling together in a wrinkle at the power of my screams. Like all toddlers everywhere, I searched for the parent who wasn't currently holding me.

"Dudesy," I wailed in the general vicinity of the front door as if I could summon him.

"Dude's gone, baby," Mom said on a repressed sigh. "I'm here. Let's look at your little hand."

"I'm coming home," my mother had whispered several weeks earlier, white-knuckling the phone at her ear. "Just until I figure out what to do."

She stood in the trailer's small kitchen, waif-thin and worn through with nerves. Tekla squirmed in her arms, crying at a volume and pitch particular to colicky six-month-olds.

"Has it really gotten that bad?" Grandma asked.

Mom's lips flattened into a thinking line. There were things she couldn't say on the phone since the raid. She patted the baby's back and shuffled in place, reliving the last few months.

Dude had been a minor hustler as long as she'd known him. He wasn't a dealer, exactly, but he could get you what you needed for a party. Weed, sure. Mushrooms. Probably coke and acid with enough notice. For a while, back before she got pregnant with me, he'd thought about turning grower, but Mom said she wouldn't stick around for that.

Sometime before Christmas, though, she thought she'd noticed cars following her to and from her classes on the University of Alaska, Anchorage campus. At first, she wrote it off as paranoia. Then their mailman, a friend who regularly stopped in to smoke a joint on his lunch break, had turned up in a panic one day, saying he'd been interrogated for three hours by his boss and some detectives about what went on at our house.

"What could they want with you?" she'd asked Dude when the mailman left.

He shrugged. "I can't imagine they'd shake me down for some shitty leaf. I don't have enough to be interesting to them."

They were heading home from registering Mom for her spring courses a few weeks later when she thought she recognized a black car tucked deep in the shadows of the evergreens along our street, just off Spenard Road. It gave her pause.

"Let's visit the neighbors," she said. Dude swerved into a driveway up the street from ours to visit a friendly guy they knew who was more into coke than weed but still ran the same game as Dude.

Five minutes later, we were on the neighbor's couch when the front and back doors went BANG BANG BANG and blew inward. Men dressed all in black burst through, waving guns and shouting.

Several more crawled through the windows. Next thing, they had the neighbor in a back room, and we kids were in Mom's arms on the couch, screaming and shaking. Hard to say what shook us more, the cold or the terror.

"It's January!" Mom shouted at the cop nearest her. "Close the damn doors!"

We were sent home, but as our truck crept down the street toward our trailer, another neighbor waved from his window, saying, *Go back!* Red and blue lights flashed through the heavy trees around our place. Dude made a casual U-turn back toward Spenard Road and headed toward another friend's house across town.

Mom laid a hard eye on Dude and said, "What are you not telling me?" Rage left her voice tight and raspy, even as she reached to soothe us kids in the back seat.

"I don't know . . ." Dude said. "Business is picking up here and there."

"Business?"

"I've been getting some real good weed lately. Better than that leaf, you know?"

"How much are you talking about?"

He scratched his nose and shrugged. "I don't know . . . I've got maybe a pound left?" he said.

"Where is it *now*?" Mom asked.

"I mean, right *now*, it's in the truck," Dude said. "We're safe."

"Our home is being raided as we speak. You're driving your children around with a jailable amount of drugs in the truck, and you think we're safe?" Her breath boiled out in a gush of steam despite the truck's heater going full blast. "You promised you'd quit this shit." Tears in her eyes now. "I am not going to lose my kids because you won't get a real fucking job!"

A long, silent sob swelled up and through her. Another. Another. She imagined us growing up as wards of the state; our parents locked away on drug trafficking charges. She wasn't *herself* trafficking, but still. She sucked in air.

Dude reached over and slapped her. Hard. "Quit being hysterical," he said, each of the twenty years between them ringing in his deep baritone voice.

"I can't raise my kids like this," Mom said, switching the phone to her other ear. "The cops always sniffing around, strangers at the door day and night. I'm exhausted."

"It's not only the partying," she said. "The house is a hazard. I used to think he was just messy, you know? So I tried to get rid of some of the garbage, clear up enough space to live in . . ." Even then, Dude's home was scarier than Ariel's little cave of worthless wonders. Bags of garbage and collectibles lined furniture, floor, and kitchen counters with equal disregard. Yellowed receipts and expired calendars covered the walls while stacks of empty beer cans and liquor bottles lined the halls. He could not be convinced to part with a thing, and he knew where every single item belonged in any given pile. It troubled my mother deeply. A child could lose herself any number of ways in that tiny trailer.

That had worked to Dude's advantage when the cops raided the place. They hadn't found anything incriminating enough in the trailer to warrant a seizure or a second raid. They'd have needed a year to hunt through it all and find the letters from a dealer in Hawaii, or the loose nuggets of bud and leaf squirreled away in tattered bags, and two or three marijuana plants he had growing in a kitchen bursting with random plants of all shapes and sizes under a shared heat lamp. Never mind the rolls of cash stashed randomly in shoes and mittens, stuffed inside full rolls of toilet paper, and buried in coffee cans with the coffee beans still in them. Ultimately, they hadn't found what they were looking for because it had been in the back of the truck with us.

By pure luck, we'd been in the wrong house at the right time, and the whole thing had just barely passed us by.

Almost. Because the close call had brought with it a revelation: despite his promises, Dude would never change. Not for my mother. Not for us kids. The trailer that had once been a sanctuary of love and childbirth and music now closed in on her, squeezing the breath from her body as she laid with us girls at night.

She'd begun taking us out all day and carefully marking every car on the street when she returned. She obsessively watched the street outside through a crack in the blinds and refused to open the door to anyone she didn't recognize, realizing as she did so how many more strangers had been visiting in recent months.

She cleaned while we napped, desperate for something she could control. Even there she was stymied. "You can't just throw perfectly good newspapers away," Dude raged, dumping ten years of Anchorage Daily News back issues out of the garbage bin. "And these milk jugs. I might need them one day!"

Mom sighed into the phone. "I've got our tickets," she told Grandma. "We'll be home tomorrow." After the raid, she'd waited four months for things to settle down, longer than she thought she could ever live with the kind of worry she now owned. Finally, she'd packed our things and told Dude we were off to visit her mother in Petersburg. The tickets were one-way.

Back home in Petersburg, Mom's younger siblings, Toby, Rocky, and Jolette, were still in high school. She worried at the legacy her oldest brother, Buck, had left behind with his small-town thuggery, drugs, and womanizing. Toby and Rocky seemed on the verge of following in his footsteps. Grandma worked long hours running the local shipyard and a curio store downtown that she owned called The Star.

Mom had finally escaped the chaos of Dude's home only to find herself once again up to her elbows in dishes and laundry and the business of raising her younger siblings, plus now her own children. She couldn't be sure from day to day whether she'd sailed into safe harbor or a recurring nightmare.

When I imagine a real-life Cinderella in this non-magical world, I think of my mother. She might have been the third child of six, but she was the first girl. For all of her short existence, the heavy chores had fallen her direction: cooking, sewing, cleaning, laundering, bandaging, comforting, and biting back the shame each time her oldest brother threatened her into submission when no one was looking. She had married as a teenager to escape it all, and now here she was a few short years later: a divorcee with two girls from yet another failed partnership. Back where it all began.

Mom took a waitressing job at Sandy's Cafe downtown, despite offers from Grandma to work at The Star or the shipyard. She had school friends in Petersburg but mostly kept to herself outside of work. Two kids, a half-finished art degree, and a sore heart seemed like enough trouble, she said. She accepted flirtations and tips with equal aplomb but passed on dates and parties. There were a few boys who wanted to change that, she knew. Thom in particular, but he ran in the same troubled circles as her brothers.

Thom stumped into the diner with those steel-toed logging boots every morning, his mustache a black dash above full lips and a promise in his eyes. Every morning she brought him waffles with strawberries and shook her head. *No*, she wouldn't go out with him tonight. She had a future in mind: finish that art degree, set up a good home for her girls, maybe play cello with the local symphony again. At the time, Thom could barely rub two vowels and a consonant together.

"You can rebuild an engine, and you can read, but you can't write?" she'd said, refilling his coffee.

"I don't need to write to see how parts go together," he'd shrugged. Maybe he wasn't a deep intellectual, but he had a kindness and strength under all that wild small-town boy that she found comforting.

She said no so often she finally said yes to put an end to it.

She brought him home to meet us after the second date, thinking we'd scare him away. Instead, I showed him the blisters from the black stove on my right hand, spanning the length of the first three fingers and across my palm. He pulled me into his lap, looked hard at the fat white bubbles, and kissed them all. "I think you're going to be just fine," he said with a hitch in his voice. All my life, I've judged the worth of a man on his ability to feel the small sorrows of a child.

Sometimes when he visited, we said, "Dudesy!" and he'd hunker down on the floor to look us in the eyes. "Girls, I'm not your father. I'm not Dude." Then he'd carry us into the hall, one in each arm, to point out a photograph. "That's your father," he'd say, finger pressed to the image of a huge bearded man with eyes as blue as forget-me-nots under bushy red eyebrows.

Dude came for us, of course. He called from the airport, a dirt airstrip on the edge of town.

"I'm afraid Fawn's at work," Grandma said through a crack in the door, stalling.

"Oh, that's fine," Dude said as if he'd been invited for tea and had nowhere else to be anyway. "I'm just here to bring everyone home."

I owned none of the apprehension my grandmother felt when she swung the door wide to let him in. I saw only my father, none of the worry. I climbed his thick legs like a mountain, screaming to be held, and laughed as he carried us out to the backyard to romp in the grass.

Since he'd last seen us, Tekla had mastered the crawl, learned to drag herself to her feet using furniture, and started on that shaky baby two-step that goes *one*, *two*, pause, repeat. He took us out back to watch her practice those jerky little steps. When she tired, we sprawled on Dude's chest like a living room rug, one child's head for each half of his heart. I breathed him in, wrinkling my nose. "You stink," I said. And promptly fell asleep.

I still don't know how anyone convinced him to leave without us.

"He'll take the girls," Mom said to Thom after Dude left. "I don't know how, but he will." It twisted her guts. She wanted us to know our father, but she worried at the prospect of our future with him. She chain-smoked while pacing the back deck and painting furiously for several days.

She painted in watercolors. The marina, boats, people, the view from Grandma's porch with its too-white railings and creeping flowerpots, the sweep of lawn drifting towards the harbor. A wide sky somewhere out there, waiting.

At night she crawled into bed with us and sang in a voice so whisper soft that you had to concentrate to hear it. The effort of listening knocked us right out. She laid with us long hours, watching the ocean swell through the window, wondering how long it would be before Dude returned.

A month later, we piled into Thing, Thom's 1971 blue Dodge van with no back seats. We boarded a ferry bound for Sheldon Jackson College in Sitka, where maybe Dude wouldn't find us for a while. Mom took art classes, and Thom ferried back and forth from Petersburg. Mom coached him in reading and writing when he visited. We settled into a rainy routine.

Winter in Southeast Alaska is *wet*, and Sitka is no exception. The small city clings to the shoreline like a barnacle, the perpetually lapping waters lending a romantic feel to all kinds of weather. Even the grocery store parking lot offers stunning views of the sun rising and setting over the bowled crest of Mount Edgecumbe, the dormant volcano on nearby Kruzof Island. Through the dark months, a white mantle glows atop nearby mountain peaks but rarely is it cold enough for snow to cling to the rocky beaches for longer than a week.

During visits, Thom drove us girls out of town to traipse through the red cedars, Sitka spruce, and hemlocks of the Tongass National Forest and to watch whales fattening up for winter from the shore.

Around Christmas, doubt set in. "They ought to hear your voice at least," Mom said when Dude answered on the sixth ring. Adding, "No, you can't visit. We don't have room for you."

He came anyway, staying for several weeks that time.

"We're not going back to Anchorage," Mom told him. "I'm in school. The kids are happy; they love Thom. This is where we're going to be."

"Guess I'm moving to Sitka." Dude said.

Thom was in Petersburg for work, or he might have intervened. Mom, alone, felt helpless to dissuade Dude when he flew home to gather a few belongings.

That was it for Sitka. We left before Dude could return to find us that Christmas. We ferried to Bellingham and then drove on to Pendleton, Oregon, where Mom and Thom enrolled in the Blue Mountain Community College.

It wasn't smooth sailing. Despite his lack of education, Thom had the first and final word on everything. "Well, you see, Fawn," he'd say, and then follow up with something like, "the education system is designed to make artists feel worthwhile, but the real world doesn't support the pursuit of Humanities. What's the point of an art degree in the modern economy?"

She had traded in the insecurity of a partner who loved the arts but refused legitimate and legal work for a partner who worked tirelessly but questioned the value of her dreams.

Thom could not carry a tune or bring the world to life with oil paints and a knife. Perhaps that's why he couldn't see how the arts defined my mother, as Dude had. I wonder how he imagined their life would be if she gave up the few things that made her feel real, and whole, and separate from the darkness of her childhood. Surely he didn't picture her at home in the kitchen, ready to serve him polite children and hot meals in the evenings? Even my imagination doesn't stretch that far.

I, on the other hand, became Thom's most devoted pupil, hungry for everything he had on offer. Nothing felt more special and good than when Thom hoisted up my tiny toddler body to listen to Thing's Slant-6 engine as he adjusted the timing. "It's important to know what a healthy engine sounds like, so you can hear when something goes wrong." Then he'd demonstrate with a screwdriver, revving the engine super high so he had to shout over the roar: "Do you think this engine should sound like that when it's idling?" Of course, I shook my head *no*.

One night at bedtime, I asked, "Is Thom my daddy now?" and Mom shook her head. "I just don't have that husband feeling about him," she told me.

"I have a daddy feeling for him," I said. "Okay?"

"He's probably a real good guy to have daddy feelings for," she said. Still, it didn't work for her the way it worked for me. Something was missing in the *'til death do us part* department.

They took walks and listened to the radio, and it was easy to have fun together. They philosophized about mortality over joints, shared a burger and a beer when they went out. They were best friends and lovers at an age, in an age, where it was generally expected to be coupled up and having kids. She felt that pressure keenly.

"Why won't you marry me?" he asked over and over. She shook her head every time, saying, "I'm not the marrying kind." She had that hippie heart still. She loved music in a minor key, paint under her fingernails, sunset with a good joint. Thom was more black-and-white, with old-school spiritual leanings and the expectations of gender roles that went with it. Why did she want to be off at school when she had children to raise and a man to care for?

Thom's eternal wisdom left her feeling hemmed in, somehow. She pined for the world she'd known: the small-town people she'd grown up with and her family, as complicated as that relationship was. Maybe she didn't know everything there was to know about engines or indoor plumbing, but she was an educated woman. She knew enough to want more.

I knew none of her apprehensions. I only knew that my very favorite thing was wrestling on the living room floor in student housing. Thom on his back, laughing, that little black mustache stretched wide on a smile, we girls tumbling over him and each other and our own two feet like crazed puppies. We rarely waited for him to line up his boots by the door before climbing him like a ladder.

"What are we gonna do tonight?" he'd say.

"Milkshakes," Tekla would say.

"Star Trek," I would say.

And that would be that.

Our love for Thom softened her, blinded her to their differences. Mom said no to marriage so often she finally said yes to put an end to the question.

Wrapping up the spring semester, she flew with us girls from Pendleton to Petersburg to plan the wedding. There she met a one-eyed artist by the name of Ray working at the airport check-in counter.

She said no to him at first, too.

The Hard One

~~~

I want to spare you this part of my story because it is dark and hard, but also because it may be difficult to believe that what happens next isn't my entire life's story. Well, in a way, it is. And in another way, it isn't. It is because it shaped me. And it isn't because what happened warped the weave, but I wove myself whole out of remnants in spite of it. I've chosen to leave this hard time here because, without it, I am incomplete. I grew up and through this the way a tree will absorb an obstacle in its path over time. I am a stubborn Sitka spruce with the bones of this story embedded in my flesh. I will show you the marks on my body. I fear them no more.

When I think back to our time with Ray, it's easiest if I put myself in my mother's shoes.

Here is Fawn, an artist with two toddler girls and big dreams. She is engaged to marry an ambitious and intelligent young man who makes her doubt everything she thinks is beautiful about herself, despite his devotion. At the airport, where she's gone to buy the groom's plane ticket north for the wedding, she meets a tall man. Thin, with dark hair and an eye patch. He's an artist too, he tells her. And a musician. He talks her into grabbing a cup of coffee at the nearby diner when he hears she has two little girls.

She sees in Ray a kindred spirit. He confesses he's always wanted a family. In fact, he has a big old house in Washington, an inheritance, just waiting for him to fill it with laughter. They talk about art and love, and being misunderstood. She says no to dinner so many times she finally says yes, and soon she's on the phone with her fiancé, calling off the wedding.

"What about the girls?" Thom asks.

"It's me you want to marry," she tells him. "You don't understand *me*."

We didn't return to Oregon in the fall after leaving Petersburg but moved to Ray's hometown, Bremerton, Washington, instead. Mom transferred her student loans to the community college there and put money down on an apartment, refusing to move in with Ray at first. "It's just for now," she told him. He had a habit of sulking that unnerved her.

An article had run in the local paper shortly after our move, announcing a new Sex Offender/Crimes Against Minors registry in Seattle. "It's about damn time," she said to Ray, who sat silent on the couch a long time before replying.

"Sometimes kids are sexy, though," he said, finally. "They just act sexy. Don't you think?"

"What the hell are you talking about?" she said, afraid her trembling tongue might give her away. "Kids don't know what sexy even means." She'd carried the secret of her childhood so long she didn't know how to give voice to it.

He'd stalked out of the house then.

He became morose after that, mopey even. He'd visit and sit on her couch in the darkest corner, staring at the ceiling for hours on end. Years later, she tells me she worried that he'd suspected her secret. That he resented her, thought her tainted. She thanked her lucky stars she'd had girls. No sons to do to us what her brother had done to her. No crazy family to endanger us.

After a couple of months, Mom drove to Oregon to pick up our belongings, leaving us with Ray for the handful of days it took to gather what little we had in storage. Thom had agreed to help her bring our things to Bremerton. He loved her, even then.

"Thom was sad," she says. "He missed us. But I think he understood why I felt like I belonged with someone more like me."

I remember those days we were left with Ray with the accuracy of a three-year-old child:

Gray light filters through a high, square window at the end of the bedroom Tekla and I share. The pillow I lie on is soaked through with tears. I am on the top bunk in our small bedroom, shivering and crying silently, while Tekla, in the bunk below, screams the kind of scream that makes your own throat hurt just listening. At daycare in Petersburg, they'd called her The Screamer for her fits. This isn't the same thing, and I know it. At three years old, I don't understand most of what Ray says, only the cruelty of it:

You think you're so sexy, don't you? Walking around like you own the world.

I see the way you look at me.

Think you're smart? Thought I wouldn't notice you?

You are nothing, and no one cares what happens to you.

The gun he shows me is black as the patch over his left eye, and the smell of it makes my nose curl when he wands it over my body, head to toe. I know without a doubt what he means when he presses the gun to my temple and says:

If you tell your mother, I will kill her.

I choose not to remember the feel of his hands on me. I don't remember pain. The memories are there but consciously muted. I've learned what I can from them by now. I don't need them anymore. Instead, I remember mostly that I wanted to climb from my bunk into Tekla's and hold her until Mom came back from wherever she'd gone, and we were safe.

When Ray finally left us a few days later, I clamped my jaws against the possibility of his return, readying myself to bite his throat out. I knew he would kill me for trying. I think I even grasped the concept of death, then. Of nothingness. I yearned for it plenty in those days. I knew it for a price I would gladly pay if I could save my sister one more moment of pain.

Though I never saw him again, it took thirty years, two broken teeth, and thousands of dollars in mouthguards before I finally loosened my grip on his throat.

Mom and Thom returned to our apartment in Bremerton to find the door wide open, lights off. No Ray. No kids. No note. There was no answer at Ray's, or their old boss's house, or our downstairs neighbor's. "Where are my fucking children?" Mom screamed out the window.

"Someone must know *something*," Thom said. They raced through the neighboring apartment buildings, Mom weeping and pounding bruises into her fists on every door until she heard Tekla wailing in a nearby apartment.

"I found them wandering around," the neighbor lady said. She was a total stranger. "They were just filthy. All dirty diapers, screaming hungry, and nobody there with them. I didn't know where they came from." It's anyone's guess how long we'd been left there, alone in the apartment, before we made our way outside.

At first, I didn't say anything because at night I heard Ray in my head saying, *If you tell your mother, I will kill her.* Sometimes I heard him so clearly, I had to stare into the darkness of our room until all the shadows made sense, and I knew for sure none of them could be him.

All my life, I'd had two speeds: overdrive and dead asleep. Now I had only one: half awake. I stopped talking and turned my nose up at food. I made a pile of the few stuffed toys I owned and slept nestled in them all day. I went back to wearing diapers. When Mom put me to bed, I crawled from my top bunk into Tekla's and lay all night, inhaling her milky breath, lulled by the quiet comfort of her baby snores.

Imagine my mother's bewilderment.

We still had a few things of Ray's, like the nice white Formica table their former boss had given him, for instance. Shouldn't he at least come back for that? What had she done to drive him away?

She asked me again and again, *Did something happen?* I only shook my head, burrowing deeper into my stuffed army.

Her hands shook as she raised the phone to her ear, calling everyone she knew in Bremerton, painfully few people. Great dark bruises spread from her eyes to her cheeks. She stopped painting, skipped class, hovered over me while I slept. I could feel her there, on the other side of my eyelids.

How I ache for the power to turn back time so that I could hold my mother through the horror of those early days.

"Something bad happened, Mother," she told Grandma over the phone the day after they found us. "I don't know what's going on." So Grandma flew down from Petersburg and flipped a loophole switch in my brain.

First thing Grandma did was smother me between her huge perfumed breasts. Then she took me to the store for bread.

She wheeled me around in the cart, quietly talking. "You've been pretty tired lately, haven't you?" I said nothing.

"You've gone back to wearing diapers."

Silence.

"Why do you think that is?"

Then, eventually, "Is there anything you want to tell me?"

I shook my head, too scared to speak. I looked up into my grandmother's huge green eyes, so fiercely trained on mine they nearly vibrated. Something turned in my mind. He'd only told me not to tell my mother.

"He's mean," I said. "He's bad." It felt good to speak again.

I find it strange, still, that my grandmother could sit with me through that time with such an open heart, but when faced with the revelation of her own son's abuse of my mother many years later, she could not, would not, believe it.

Mom never unloaded the furniture and boxes she had brought from storage in Oregon. Instead, we all headed straight back to Pendleton, where Thom helped us find a new apartment. All through the next semester, Thom lived with his mother in Tenino, Washington, but drove five hours each way to visit us on weekends.

A month or so later, the cops came looking for that white Formica table Ray had left behind, which baffled Mom. As far as she knew, it had been given to them by their old boss, and she couldn't fathom getting the cops involved. What if police scrutiny meant she lost us? The world had not prepared my mother for con artists and pedophiles outside of her own family. Until Ray, the safest people in the world had always been anyone she wasn't connected to by blood. Now she feared judgment for her failure to recognize danger and protect us.

When the cops asked why Ray had disappeared, left his things with her, she said they'd had differences. They'd fought, and he'd left. Old story. Hard to refute. How could she tell the police that she'd left her girls with a new boyfriend in order to break up with her fiancé?

Thom sent Mom out for coffee.

What scorching rage he must have felt as he sat in that interrogation room. How weighty his sorrow.

As the door snicked shut behind my mother, he turned burning eyes on the officers and laid out the facts. In return, they shared with him what they'd stirred up: Ray had a whole pile of aliases, multiple arrests, and may or may not have been wanted in as many as fourteen states. But you can hardly graduate from police academy without learning to recognize a parent set on vengeance, and after the initial tidal wave of information, we never discovered anything more about the man we knew of as Ray.

I imagine how it must have felt for my mother returning home to us with that knowledge, a lifetime of heartache for her two little girls stretching out before her. She might have been surprised by the tight circle of our arms when she found us curled up on the couch together in matching dresses sewn by her own hands. We were one person with two bodies breathing softly in sync.

I picture my mother gathering us into her lap, inhaling our barely-more-than-baby smell, and I can only wonder at the worry she'd accumulated since leaving Anchorage. The ghosts of her own childhood whispering, *You were supposed to protect them.*

I only began to piece it all together in my late twenties. The events around that time remain fragmented, the timeline imprecise. Even my own memories are hard to pin down. As for my mother, imagine your grown child asking you for the particulars of an episode no other adult witnessed, the anguish of so many unanswerable questions. Still, I'm thankful for my mother's strength and her willingness to look hard at that time of our lives with me. I could have been left alone with my memories the way she had been.

When asked, two decades later, Thom first said, "Are you sure you want to dig into this? Some things are better left alone," and Mom said, "It's complicated. Ray groomed us all so thoroughly I couldn't tell you if the sun was out or the stars during those few months we were together."

We had talked about it a lot in the early years, though, on the advice of a family therapist. "Do you remember Ray?" Mom would ask. Sometimes I did. Sometimes I didn't admit it. Always, though, exhaustion overwhelmed me when I heard his name, a heavy-eyed paralysis that left me feeling impossibly unreal. "The therapist said we couldn't let you bury it," Mom told me years later. But Grandma, who didn't yet know about her own daughter's torments, worried about dwelling on it too much, lest we become obsessed with it and never let it go. Talk about it, she said. Just not too much.

Despite everyone's efforts, the facts scrambled. The more I tried to explain to myself how we wound up with Ray, the more things went fuzzy. As the years passed, I heard mixed stories from family members. I confused movie plots with reality. I filled in the blanks, as children do.

For a long time, I thought Ray was a drug dealer, that my mother had left us with him to pick up a shipment of weed from her brother in Petersburg. I thought she had already married Thom and was having an affair with Ray. I thought it happened in Portland because we were in Washington so short a time I don't recall the streetlights of Bremerton, whether there are mountains there or if it rains half the year. I thought Ray had been a bad guy through and through. I thought Mom had known it and left us with him anyway. This is the faulty logic of a child, and there is no cure for the regret of it.

I will never know who I might have been without Ray in my story, but it's not hard to guess at the sorrows I'd have owned without my mother there to help me carry the memory of him. I'm thankful for that. She knew what silence could do to a person.

"This too shall pass," Mom said when the weight of it all drew our heads to her shoulders. Then she gathered us girls in until we were a mess of heartbeats and legs, tangled roots reaching down into the warmth of her. "My arms are big enough to hold us all until then."

We grew up together in that way.

And Then There Were Three

~~~

"I do," Mom said, smiling up at Thom. The Justice of the Peace nodded, and Mom looked at Tekla and me with a silent giggle. We giggled back.

After Ray had disappeared, Thom did what he'd always done: he kept showing up. He persisted in loving us. All of us. He was reliable as well-worn shoes, a steadfast friend. She still worried that maybe a strong friendship might not be enough for a strong marriage, but without him, she was alone with this new hurt in her life. Now they were comrades, warriors in the battle to protect us girls.

Thom had spent so many weekends stopping in to check on us that eventually, he just stayed. By the next Christmas, we were one big family again. Then two cells became four, became eight, sixteen, thirty-two until eventually, they blossomed into a big ol' belly full of brother. When Mom married Thom the following summer, I could finally get serious about my daddy feelings for him.

We spent a lot of time at the midwife's farm that spring, often driving to her place for long weekends. On every visit, Mom arrived tired-eyed, her olive skin dulled to a lusterless yellow. Sheri fed her plate after plate of wholesome, vegetarian farm food; buckwheat pancakes, hearty soups, vegetables and potatoes, and goat milk.

The midwife had chickens, which Tekla and I mostly ignored until the day all of their eggs hatched at once. We gathered as many chicks as we could carry in our arms, pressing our cheeks to their yellow chests while they *cheep, cheep, cheeped* to be let free. Those featherlight babies cracked open a fragile, aching wonder in me as jagged as the shells they'd left behind. I could not get enough of that feeling. We romped in the hen house daily until a chick jumped free from one of our arms and died beneath our feet.

"You can't play with the chicks until they're bigger," Mom said after that. "They're just teeny-tiny babies."

While Sheri kept us kids busy helping with the animals, Mom slept in late and read books in the hammock. She didn't have to bother with even so much as thinking her way through breakfast planning. With the hens and horses and goats to feed, the blackberries and strawberries and grapes to gorge on, and an endless pile of downy clouds to throw our imaginations into, we girls hardly needed her at all.

Despite the many distractions and extra hands to keep us occupied, Tekla and I frequently wandered out to the hammock to check in with Mom.

"What'cha doing?" we'd ask.

"Oh, just blossoming on the vine," she'd say on a sleepy breath, turning a page in her book.

And it was true. By the end of each stay, you could only look at Mom and marvel at the transformation. After three days of sun and food and rest, the freckles on her forearms burned golden to the point of radiance.

"I love your summer stardust," I'd say, as Tekla and I traced shapes in a leg dangling from the hammock.

"You have them too," she'd say, pulling us up into the hammock with her. Sure enough, we did—a paler version of her smooth, dusky sky. We'd sit there for entire long minutes, pressing our arms together so tight with hers that we became the entire galaxy.

~

Thom has never been graceful when forced to idle. First thing when we arrived at Sheri's, he'd look for an engine or a water heater or a tractor to fix. But on one visit, there wasn't a project to be found, and it set his gears to grinding. After we'd polished off breakfast and wrapped up the animal feedings, I invited him to join me in a high stakes game of hide-and-seek in the barn, but he said, "I think today I'm going to see what kind of trouble I can get into with a horse."

He said *trouble* as if to mean *fun*, which is how he wound up riding the midwife's horse down to the river, where it bucked him off and stomped almost clean through his face.

I missed the midwife's warning, but I heard Mom say, "Just steer clear of the river, Thom. You heard what she said." And then he came back a long time later with the right side of his face busted open so you could see there were teeth missing right through the hole in his cheek. He tried to explain, but he made as much sense as a man with a mouthful of river pebbles. The look on Mom's face said, *If you were my child, I'd have you over my knee so fast you'd get whiplash.* I thumbed the faded white scars on my right hand and watched Thom try to work his jaw around, confusion drawing his brows into a wobbly line.

I sat in the backseat behind Thom during the long drive to the hospital, nervous and excited by the hole in his cheek. Because what is more exciting to a toddler than a grotesque accident that requires a midnight car ride? I might have felt differently had I known that Thom would be thin as a dying man soon. Or that, between the advanced pregnancy and a husband slowly starving to death, things were going to get hard for Mom. Soon I would be sent to stay with Grandma in Petersburg for a while.

I didn't know those things, though. I felt only excitement on our late-night drive. Mostly because I could see inside Thom's face, and I liked car rides, and when Thom pulled the towel away from his cheek, I could see his teeth grinning through the hole by the green light of the dashboard.

Two months later, the wires were off and the stitches removed, and Thom was finally eating solid food again. We drove all afternoon through August heat, winding up the coast from Oregon to Seattle. Mom climbed out of the car, stretched her back, and moaned, her great big baby belly bumping into the open door. I looked over at Tekla asleep on the backseat as I slid out. Leaving her behind put an ache in me I couldn't name.

I wanted to climb back into the car and pull all of the doors shut, to close that safe shell tight around my family and return immediately home to the bed I knew, the people I belonged to.

I reluctantly accepted Mom's hand and followed her into the place where Grandma was staying. The plan was for Grandma and me to fly to Petersburg that afternoon, where I would stay for a month and return to the midwife's farm around the baby's due date. Instead, Mom went into labor before they even crossed the state line back into Oregon. She delivered Camden at a tiny roadside clinic in Proser, Washington.

There were two doctors on call at the little clinic, but the baby drew his first breath before either one could be summoned.

I imagine Thom swaddling the baby in the dim light and laying him on Mom's belly before covering them both with an additional blanket. Intentional and slow, exactly as he'd rehearsed it with the midwife. How he must have prayed his way through that premature delivery in that strange, dark room. Even the steadiest hand might shake under such circumstances.

Then came the doctor and a fight over the lights, and the doctor's shock at Camden lying there in the swaddling clothes with his belly bulging. Under the blanket, the doctor discovered a pile of intestines sprouting from the baby's midsection, clinging desperately to the umbilical cord. *Gastroschisis*, it's called. A rare birth defect barely understood at the time.

A special neonatal crew from a neighboring city whisked Mom and the baby to another hospital in Yakima, but the doctors insisted nothing could be done for him unless he made it to Swedish Children's Hospital in Seattle. A jet snatched Mom and the baby into the air and flew west, back to Seattle, where Grandma and I had delayed our flight north for a day, just in case.

Camden underwent his first surgery at eight hours old. Eventually, the twisted knot of stitches where his belly button should have been would fade to white and harden. As he grew older, we would blow raspberries on the pink scar that remained and call it his zipper. But in the early days, that wound was just more heartache and worry in a young mother's life already full-up with hand wringing.

I very much did not want to go to Alaska anymore. Still, we boarded our flight to Petersburg the next morning as planned. Grandma gently urged me on, even as confused tears dropped freely from my chin to the careless grey floor of the jetway.

Quiet, Child

~~~

Grandma liked to sing show tunes while putting on her face in the morning. The louder and more operatic, the better. And she enjoyed having an audience. "*Keema Mariaaaaaa*," she'd sing, summoning me from my bowl of oatmeal in the kitchen. I was accustomed to living life at high volume, and without my sister's constant bellowing, I found the quiet of Grandma's house in Petersburg unnerving. Opera mornings were a nice break from the monotony.

"There you are, darling," Grandma would say at my arrival, waving her arms with a dramatic flourish. "It's a great morning for a little *Cabaret*, don't you think?"

She wore her nails long and red, rings on each finger, and a gold nugget on a thick gold rope at her neck. The gold bracelets up and down both of her forearms chimed like fairy song, and the perfumes of her boudoir made my throat burn, but I sat as expected on the king-sized bed to watch her in bra and nylons as she lined her eyes and lips. Then she ratted out her hair with a fine comb until it formed a snarled halo around her face.

Back home, Tekla and I wore matching homemade clothes that Mom scratched out of second-hand women's dresses. Our house was always clean, if artistically threadbare. Among our used furniture, there was nothing glittery and nothing extra; no footrests or figurines. When Mom read stories about castles and magical kingdoms, I always thought of Grandma's house.

Now that I had Grandma's fancy house to myself, all I could think of was how much I missed our ratty couch. I ached for my mother's coffee kisses and my sister's ear-splitting screams. I'd have gladly traded this great adventure for a book in my mother's lap.

I wanted to dress up with Grandma in the mornings but had only the one forbidden dress she'd given me early on during that visit: a rose-colored satin affair with antique ivory lace and little rosebuds on the creamy ribbon. It had been made just for me in my role as a flower girl for a friend of Grandma's and was, as far as I understood, the actual reason for my visit. Camden's early arrival had simply extended it.

I generally didn't mind being a girl so much unless I was expected to be *girly*. Lace and ribbons and manners made me itchy. But for a short while, nothing in the world seemed as beautiful as that dress. I wore it only once, for the wedding, where everyone called me darling, precious, and precocious. I thought precocious was the same as precious.

"Was I good, Grandma?" I asked at the end of the ceremony.

"Perfect."

"Am I pretty, Grandma?" I twirled so the dress flared like a rose gold bell.

"You look *gorgeous*, dah-link!"

The next morning when Grandma turned from the mirror to ask, "Well, what do you think?" I said, "Grandma, you look *gorgeous*, dah-link!" And lo, her nickname came to be.

Sometimes when Grandma Gorgeous Darling went to work, I snuck into her closet to put my dress on. I powdered my cheeks with whatever I could find, pulled stringy orange hair from my face, and danced around Grandma's enormous perfumed bedroom. I'd have preferred another kid to dress up with, but it passed a little time at least. I couldn't imagine being an only child forever.

My aunt Jolette was sixteen years old and a sophomore in high school. She wore her blonde hair curled, and her white eyelashes painted black. In the mornings, she pinched her cheeks pink before dressing me up in Grandma's bright silk scarves.

"Let's walk!" she'd say.

Some days we walked for hours. Up and down the streets we went, waving at boats in the harbor, petting neighborhood dogs, and admiring the bright magenta flowers in every window box in town.

Jolette carried me on her hips and her shoulders, swung me by my legs, upside down and laughing. She pushed a borrowed stroller along the docks and giggled when tourists from the cruise ships asked: "Is she yours?"

"No," she said, but her hand on mine said *yes*, and for a few minutes, I could forget the constant ache that pulsed in my chest like a bruise that would not heal. Grandma reminded me that with the baby coming so early and needing so much care, it would be too hard on Mom to send me home right away. Still, I pined.

I watched Jolette practice cheers in front of the kitchen window after school, so big and so black on a cloudy night you might mistake it for a portal to another world. I danced along, pretending Tekla was out there looking in, trying to get through to me.

Jolette liked tucking me into bed. "Aunty," I said on my first night there, blankets up to my chin, "I love you so much." I wrapped my arms around her neck and held fast. I had only ever slept with my sister beside me. I didn't know how to do it without her. I aimed a shot of blue eyes and extra special sweetness at Jolette, suckering her into laying with me in my room until I fell asleep, a trick I employed every night thereafter.

My uncle Rocky also still lived at home. Two years older than Jolette, Rocky had dark Mason eyes like my mother, and he whistled like it was his life's business whenever he was home. This is a very important skill I might never have learned if it weren't for his amazing talent and ceaseless application of the whistle to any situation. When I cried, he whistled like a bird. When I was happy, he whistled show tunes. When I scraped my knee, he whistled mindlessly while covering me in bandages.

"Like this, kid," he said, rounding his lips into a tiny "O" and trilling like a foreign songbird. At first, the most I could do was a purr with my lips out in the smooch position, but I managed to send out a small tweet by the end of my stay.

I could have listened to him all day and all night. But Uncle Rocky had far too busy a social life for my liking and was hardly ever home.

Days grew lonelier still when Rocky and Jolette went back to school. Grandma's house was white with a pink roof and chandeliers all over. She had too many nice things for my comfort. China dolls, lace doilies, statues, and great big paintings of polar bears and storm-tossed ships. And rules. So many rules. Play quietly, be polite, no roughhousing.

Grandma's house in Petersburg didn't match the stories I'd heard from Mom's youth out on the homestead in Portage, where they'd lived in a pair of ancient pull-along campers connected by a lean-to. The kids were left to themselves during the week while Grandma worked an hour away in Anchorage and kept an apartment of her own. The older boys, Buck and Neal, were gone by then, leaving my thirteen-year-old mother to manage the chores and mind her three younger siblings alone. By then, she'd been toting buckets of water, stoking fires, laundering clothes, cooking over a wood stove, and raising kids for more than half her life.

"If our clothes were dirty or the beds unmade when my mama got home on Friday night, she'd beat us all blue," my mother told me many times. This hadn't fired me up about putting my own clothes away, but it had given me an appreciation for the lack of beatings in my daily life.

Now Grandma owned the kind of house where mirrors hung on every wall. Great big heavy things with elaborate gold frames. Occasionally I'd walk into a room, and my reflection would catch me off guard. Tangle-haired and spindly, I looked like the kind of kid who'd get kicked out of a place as fine and special as Grandma's.

It was enough to make my four-year-old body shiver with pent-up energy even as I tried like hell not to do anything to unleash Grandma Gorgeous Darling's fury. In my first week there, I'd knocked a china plate loose from a wall hanging as I caromed around the house, and she had roared, "You keep yourself to yourself, or I'll beat you 'til the blood runs and drips," and after that, I found myself too cowardly to test those red waters.

Most days, I sat for hours talking to the china dolls up on their shelves without even touching them, wishing more than ever for my plain, noisy, not-so-scary home. I didn't know how to be a quiet child. What good is a magic fairy castle if you can't even play in it?

"What if Tekla doesn't remember me, Aunty?" I asked the night before I flew home. I pulled her face close to mine and stared hard into her jeweled eyes, forbidding myself to shed the tears tickling at the back of my eyeballs.

"You're pretty hard to forget," she said, pulling the blanket over my shoulders.

Still, I worried. I owned a small, nervous apprehension that it would be easy to forget a kid like me. I was a kid you could send away in the first place.

I spied Thom through the car window when we pulled up, standing in a yard bedecked with bright orange and yellow leaves. Mom stood next to him with a bundle in her arms and the strain of sleepless nights hardening the lines of her face. Tekla squatted in the leaves in a pink coat, identical to the one I wore. She heard me pounding on the window and stood, holding out a bright red maple leaf, mouth open on a toothy smile. She did a little foot-stomping dance, and a vagrant tendril of wind swept the leaf from her hand, but she cared not at all. She ran toward me as I spilled out of the car.

"Sissie!" I said.

"Sissie!" she said.

We met in the middle of the yard, wrapped our arms around each other's necks, and didn't let go. Mom stretched out a hand for us, and I pulled her in so I could hug them both, her happiness thrumming through my chest on a long sigh.

In that moment, our first reunion, I felt my mother there beside me—my new brother in her arms with a thatch of hair as red as a blister, my sister's cheek against mine—and knew myself to be home. Next to that, nothing else in the world mattered to me as much as the divot in Tekla's chin, our secret sister-language, the little bones in her neck against the scars on my palm when I hugged her. I knew I would not sleep alone again for a long time.

Mom carried us into the house like that, all wrapped up in each other.

Switcheroo

~~~

"Ouch!" I whimpered.

"I'm sorry," Mom said, dragging the wet brush through my hair again.

I sucked air through my teeth. "It's way too tight!" I leaned back into the ankle-length dress drawn taut between Mom's knees and scratched at my scalp, trying to loosen places where my hair felt like it might rip free. "I want to wear pants," I said, staring down at the matching beige dress I wore. "This thing is ugly."

Mom sighed and waved a can of Aqua Net over my head, pressing unruly baby hairs flat. We'd been trying out the Pentecostal Church for most of the winter, but instead of filling me with the love of God, Sunday school filled me with unanswered questions. I couldn't fathom a God who let little kids suffer, and my teacher had clearly begun to despair of my why's because her friendly smile always went flat at the sight of me now.

"Thom really likes this church out of the ones we tried," Mom said. "And isn't the minister nice?"

I shrugged. The week before, when people had started weeping and talking in tongues, I had decided to try it out. Afterward, when the minister asked had I felt the Spirit, I'd said, "No, mostly just tired."—which sums up entirely my feelings about God.

I could tell Mom chafed under this new church life, too. That afternoon, as our car wound up the dusty hill toward our apartment building, she'd said, "Everyone is so nice, Thom, that's not what I'm saying. It's just . . . church three times a week is a lot. And I'm never going to stay home and keep having babies like the other wives while you're out doing your thing. I've been serving other people hand-and-foot all my life. I'm not about to do it until I die."

"Aw," Thom said, "it wouldn't be as bad as all that."

In addition to church, Thom had developed a thing for race cars. He liked to take us kids down to the local track and say things like, "You know what kind of engine that thing runs?" and, "I'd love to take that one out for a test drive." Sometimes he wasn't talking about cars, but I wasn't supposed to know that.

It became apparent that we wouldn't be able to recover financially from Thom's jaw surgery and Camden's birth if we stayed in Oregon without friends or family to help out. So Mom returned to Alaska with all three of us kids, to Ketchikan, where Grandma had opened a new curio store. Mom had family to live with and a job already waiting. Thom stayed behind in Oregon to try his hand at building and racing his own cars.

The city of Ketchikan slides down off the surrounding mountains into the Tongass Narrows so steeply that much of the downtown area is built on docks jutting out into the water and paved over. Houses were old and damp, even then. The streets narrow. The wet smell of ocean and rainforest put a joy in me I couldn't name, even as Grandma grumbled at the moss bunched up in the rooftop and lining the cracks in her sidewalks. I'd never loved lichen more than when we first returned home to the Southeast.

Thom showed up five or six months after us with a pocket full of fresh debt and no immediate prospects for curing that problem. Mom, meanwhile, was making a relative mint under the table as a housekeeper for the rich people on the hill. Thom sat around all day for the first few weeks, listless and cranky, until he landed a job at the Union 76 gas station across town and, Mom suspected, a girlfriend at the nearby pizza place.

"Maybe he resents me a little for calling off the wedding the first time," she told Aunty Jolette. "Maybe he just didn't want to move back to Alaska."

He took to coming home from work to play with us kids and eat dinner, leaving as soon as we were in bed, then returning in the morning before our alarm went off. I only realized things were bad when his staying-gone periods stretched to days and ended with a hurt in Mom's voice that we could hear even with the door shut.

It got so I started whining the moment Thom reached for his coat. "Why do you have to leave?" I'd complain.

"I have to work, kiddo," he'd say, tugging on his huge boots while I chewed an imaginary hangnail just to work a little blood loose.

"It's Saturday! You should get to stay home with us," I'd say.

"That's not how jobs always work." He'd pull me onto his lap and drag a hand through my hair. "You've got to stop terrorizing your fingernails," he'd say, examining my fingers. I still had the scar across my palm, the one I'd shown him the very first time we met. He'd kiss my bleeding fingers and be gone, just like that. My fingers were already back in my mouth before the door closed as I worry, worry, worried at the dry, torn flesh.

I wondered if he knew how shaky I felt when he left.

In the spring, Mom ferried to Petersburg for her tenth high school reunion. The ferry was a different world than the lonely place back home with Thom. Musicians gathered on the upper deck to jam and then met up for pitchers of beer in the bar while kids formed mobs and built blanket forts in one of the viewing lounges. She hadn't felt so at home in years. After that, she knew the marriage was over.

"We just don't have that married feeling," Mom told us. "It was a nice idea, but it didn't work."

I couldn't figure why Thom would let us go. He'd fought so hard to land this gig; I couldn't understand why he didn't seem to want to keep it.

As a six-year-old, what I knew of love was that it ought to form a single line. You loved a person, and that was the whole shape of it. I didn't know you could love a person but not be in love with them. Or that you could love a person and not want them in your life.

Thom's absences made me question everything I knew. I became certain that my father, Dude, had already stopped loving me since I never heard from him. Maybe Thom would too. Why else did daddies leave?

Thom took a job managing an apartment building downtown. For a while, we kids took turns between his place and Mom's, but by the end of summer, they had filed a no-contest divorce and agreed between themselves to share custody of Camden equally. Mom wanted to get back to her studies. Thom agreed to let her bring Camden with us to Juneau, where Mom enrolled at the University of Alaska, Southeast. They agreed Camden would stay with us during the school year and with Thom over summer and Christmas breaks. When he was old enough to start school, it would switch. Now it was just the four of us: Mom, Tekla, Camden, and me.

Camden was a three-year-old with the sleep habits of a bossy rooster. He particularly liked to wake up at four in the morning to flip on the lights and smash his toy cars together—an unpleasant surprise for anyone asleep in the top bunk right under that brassy light fixture—usually me.

"Can we tape the light switch down or something?" I moaned. "Or his mouth?" One night I made him sleep in the top bunk, thinking the prospect of a night-dark climb down that wobbly ladder would stop his early morning shenanigans. It deterred him not at all. The next morning found him standing under a blanket at my bedside, a grin frozen on his tiny face, eyes bulging ghoulishly.

I sighed. "Could you at least play quietly?" I asked.

He scratched lazily at the jagged line where his belly button might have been, yawned, and scrunched up his face as if pretending to think. "Naw," he said. Then he picked up a cardboard box of army guys and dumped them on the floor next to my head, yelling, "ARMAGEDDONNNNN!"

A few weeks later, he moved out of our room and into Mom's bed, and everyone slept better. Tekla and I climbed into bed with them in the mornings and took turns trying to make Mom pee her pants from laughing. The music of her laugh drew us like bears to a spawning stream. We had three mildly successful tricks: tickle the mom, tickle the brother, and fart jokes we learned at school. We were only successful once that I recall. "Oh my gosh, stop it! I really am going to pee my pants this time!" Mom said, running to the bathroom.

Camden went to daycare. Tekla and I were first and second graders at Harborview Elementary School downtown, which looked out dreamily onto the Gastineau Channel.

Juneau hugs the channel like an old friend. The downtown area is tight, with boxy two-story buildings packed close together on the main streets and houses radiating out and up the steep foothills behind it in tiers. The city follows the channel north and spreads out into the flatlands at the foot of the Mendenhall Glacier, where we lived.

Mom took classes during the day, then drove fifteen minutes into town to pick us up and fifteen minutes back out to our apartment in student housing. We'd never had a daily commute before, and I loved it entirely. Mom cranked the radio as high as it could go, and we sang together at the top of our lungs while the telephone poles sped by.

We wrestled around with Mom sometimes, and it turned out she wasn't half bad at it. Who needed a daddy anyway? Then we ate dinner on the floor, at an old Japanese table Grandma had given us, before cuddling up in a pile of pillows to read, legs and books everywhere. We pretended the floor pillows were fancy and that the lack of a couch was a choice.

We were three little peas nestled safe in our mom-shaped pod.

"Guess who's going to spend Christmas with Dad?" Mom said enthusiastically one night after dinner. We were in a cuddle puddle on the floor, as usual, each of us kids vying for the spot nearest her.

"Us!" Camden said, throwing his hands in the air.

"And you?" Tekla asked.

"Mmmmm no . . ." Mom said, shaking her head.

"Without you?" I said. You could have detonated a confetti bomb over my head, and I wouldn't have noticed; I felt that hollow.

"Without me," she said. She'd been invited to teach a music class in Fairbanks over the break, and you could see she was equal parts relieved to send us to Thom because we would not *shut up* about missing him and devastated to spend the holiday without us.

It didn't occur to her to worry. Why would she? Which made it all the more devastating when Mom came to pick us up in Ketchikan, and she found that Thom had enrolled Camden in preschool.

"Hey, he's in school now," he said, throwing his hands up. "That was the deal."

Mom fought it. Of course she did. But without a formal custodial agreement, she had no footing. Camden was safe with a parent of record, and the lawyers promised an expensive battle if she tried to fight it.

She couldn't afford a *couch*.

After that, we got Camden for summers and Christmas break, but for the rest of the year, we had a box full of tiny race cars to remind us that we were one pea short of a full pod.

The Sound of Things

~~~

Because we never stayed in one place long enough for *home* to land on a smell or fix itself to a room, it settled on a sound.

A lone alto voice rises from the living room as Mom fingerpicks her way through a favorite Bill Steins tune, "Piney River Girl."

I heard the sound of a redbird sing
And the call of a whippoorwill

The kitchen is thick with the aroma of onion and garlic, and ground beef. Tekla stands at the sink, up to her elbows in sudsy water. At the stove, I wrap up leftover enchiladas for lunch, dreading the unfinished math homework ahead of me. Tekla hums along, rinses a plate, and jumps in with her high soprano. I follow, but an octave above Mom because I don't have the knack for picking out a harmony the way Tekla does.

In the living room, Mom shifts to a low harmony, letting me drop into the melody while Tekla lays high notes over ours:

As the sun pulled over the eastern ridges
And warmed the morning hills

We don't plan. We don't rehearse. We don't say, "How 'bout some music while we do the dishes, Ma?" We are chicks in a nest. Mom chirps out a melody, and we sing it right back. Our life is a series of school days and rainy weekends in bed with books, peppered with an ongoing stream of music festivals and jam nights and gigs, where Mom plays music with an orbiting cast of stoned guitar players, serious fiddlers, and tipsy stand-up bassists. We miss a lot of school for music. Our teachers don't mind because we always turn in our homework and they couldn't stop us anyway. Whenever Mom surprise-invited us girls up on stage during a show, we'd say, "We don't know any songs." And she'd say, "What are you talking about? You've been singing these songs all your life." Then we'd lean into the mic and find our way home together, the look in Mom's eyes saying, *I wouldn't rather be anywhere else.*

Afterward, people would come up and say, "How did you teach your girls to sing like that?" Which gave Mom an opportunity to show off her gap teeth with a smile.

"I only ever taught them to listen," she'd say. "They did the rest."

Wherever we lived, you could count on Mom to leave her little black notebook of songs and a dog-eared copy of *Rise Up Singing* stacked on the coffee table. They'd lay there like a pair of well-meaning elderly aunts I couldn't shake. *You could get serious about music if you wanted to,* they seemed to say whenever I wandered past. But I'd carry on picking at a blueberry stain or digging mud out of the cuffs of my jeans because getting serious seemed like an unbearable amount of work.

I preferred the effortless way Mom dragged us into her songs by playing them over and over and over so that on the bus ride to school, I'd catch myself singing "St. James Infirmary Blues" and wondering at the heartbreak of it.

Let her go, let her go, let her go
God rest her where'er she may be

The instruments always had a corner of their own in the living room, too, where the shadows they cast could most easily scare the bejesus out of you on your way to the bathroom in the middle of the night. Mom had a cello, several guitars, a fiddle, a mandolin, and, for a few years, a hammered dulcimer. While I could pick out a tune by ear on any of them, I only ever had serious feelings for Bessie, the cello, which I blame on the fact that Mom played Bessie while pregnant with me. The first voice I ever knew was my mother's. The second was Bessie's.

Bessie stood taller than I until fifth grade. A full-sized cello with a voice so deep and rich it fell on me like a prayer. I knew the shape of her the way I knew my mother's face, and when I plucked her strings, she drew me back to my mother's belly. She tied us together. I can hear her deep voice still: Mom plucking her like a bass from her lowest growl to a high C on "Sweet Lorraine."

And each night he prays
That nobody steals her heart away

Eventually, I got my own cello. It was a cheap cast-off the music teacher at Whitecliff Elementary in Ketchikan gave to me because it looked like it had been left in a bathtub overnight. After that, playing the cello was just more homework.

"You could be great if you'd practice," my orchestra and choir teachers said. I didn't know how to say to them, *I don't want to be great. I just want to hear the pretty noise and sing when it feels right.* So I said nothing.

"Like this," she said, pressing my fingers into the shape of an A-minor chord. "Now strum from the second string."

I ran a thumb across the strings, feeling the weight of them as they sprang free, each one sending a warm buzz from the fretboard to my brain.

"Now an E," she said, moving my fingers. I aimed wide eyes at my mother and hummed, strumming again. Mom brushed a hank of long hair behind an ear and smiled all the way up to her eyes.

"Ouch." I shook my left hand, turning it up to show her the indentations on my fingertips. I sighed and slouched over the guitar. "I like singing better."

Mom nodded. "It takes hours and hours and years and years to get good on an instrument," she said. I nodded back like I had every intention of following through on that. Which, of course, I did not. "Work on going back and forth between those chords for a while," she said. Which, of course, I did because it kept her next to me where I could smell the coffee on her breath and feel the warmth of her hand on my back like a promise.

We sat on a musty couch in a windowless old house somewhere on Douglas Island. A house we lived in so short a time I can't remember the shape of it, whether there were stairs to the front door, how far it was from either the beach or the bridge spanning Gastineau Channel that delivered us daily to Juneau for school and work.

The guitar was a nameless old thing that had seen better days before my mother found it at a thrift store. Deep scratches ran the length of its back, and the decorative pattern encircling the sound hole had rubbed off. I didn't mind because the sound it made felt like campfire on a cold, starry night.

"Shoot, you could practically write a song with just those two chords," Mom said. And I have. In high school, as a lonely teen trying out heartbreak. In my twenties, when I came back to music after a decade of trying to give it up for good. Now, again, in my thirties, writing songs with my band.

This wandering heart is lonesome as a windowless room

I hear my mother and sister when a new song tugs at me. Tekla's fierce highs and my mother's crooning lows, their harmonies ghosting across state lines and time zones to find me. In those moments, I feel them out there. My heart sirens calling me home.

Hardly Big Enough to Dress

~ ~ ~

We had a rare staying-put spell during the year and a half we knew Mr. Norman, through second grade and half of third. Choir was technically reserved for third grade and up, but Tekla and I did a special audition when we first moved to Juneau; an *a cappella* duet of "When The Red Red Robin Goes Bob Bob Bobbin' Along," and Mr. Norman bob-bob-bobbed his head up and down while we sang, thumb pressed beneath his chin in thought. By then, we had been singing on stage with Mom for years.

"Can you read?" he asked when we finished. Mr. Norman dressed like a college professor in neatly pressed slacks and a button-down shirt; collar folded precisely over a soft knit sweater vest that hugged his round belly. Years later, I learned he'd retired from a life of professional music to teach part-time for the school district, but at the time, I imagined him a fixture at Harborview, as old and permanent as the gym floor.

"I've read all the Nancy Drew books," I told him, knotting strands of long red hair around my finger.

"Me too," Tekla said. "I can read."

Because library books are free and reading next to Mom was a guaranteed cuddle session, we were gifted readers for first and second graders.

"No, no," Mr. Norman waved a thick hand. "Can you read music?"

I didn't know what it meant to read music. We heard a song and sang it. Mom liked to call us "Suzuki singers" after the Suzuki Method, which trains musicians from toddlerhood by immersing them in the world of music and allowing them to develop a natural ear. The Suzuki method was Mom's big parenting hack, and she applied it liberally to all of her interests.

We didn't get an answer right away, but a few days later, Mr. Norman knelt down and looked us in the eye. "Girls," he said very seriously, "you have a gift." He laid one stout finger across his nose and tapped it. "But if I let you into my choir, you'll have to do extra work for the regular classes you'll miss in order to be here, plus extra work to catch up with the choir. Can you do that?"

Of course, we said yes. Nothing else in the world felt as good as singing with all our hearts.

Sadly, we lost Mr. Norman to yet another move, and I don't remember a lick of what he taught me about reading music. It is a recurring heartbreak common to the children of wandering musician types: it's all adventures with strangers until you meet someone extra special who drags you into their heart. Then it's all crying jags and hasty goodbyes and having yet another person to miss wherever you go next.

Mr. Norman's choir room doubled as a rec room for the latchkey kids who needed a place to hang out until their parents got off work. There were a lot of us in the '80s. For some reason, the school day ends two or three hours earlier than most working parents can get home, and there weren't a lot of afterschool programs for us back then. Kids of all ages jammed together in the choir room—a large room divided by a curtain, with the music class on one side and a play area for younger kids on the other. We mingled easily, older kids reading to littler kids, some of us playing with preschool-aged wooden kitchen sets, others reading books or doing homework for that extra hour.

With Camden gone, Mom could work part-time after her own classes. This meant that even if Tekla and I took the late bus, we still had two hours at home alone before Mom returned.

Latchkey was alright, but who wants to spend extra time at school? We much preferred going straight home, where the rules were simple. We never answered the phone unless it rang ten times, hung up, and rang ten more times. We could not play at the park, and we never answered a knock on the door unless whoever knocked said the super-secret code word: *acidophilus*. And the only person who knew the code word was Mom. That code word was so super-secret I have a hard time saying it even now.

Sometimes Mom pretended to lose her key when she got home just so she could knock awhile and get Tekla and I all riled up. We took turns pushing each other off the wood chair we used to look out of the peephole, refusing to open the door until Mom stopped goofing and got it right.

"Open sesame?" she'd try. Through the peephole, her round face and wide brown eyes zoomed in and away from the door as she rocked on her heels semi-impatiently, long dark hair hanging past her shoulders under her felted black Stetson hat. The bend of the lens gave my mother the look of an actress in an art film: tiny and beautiful and slightly strange.

"Mom, come on!" Tekla would say, "What's the *magic* word?"

"Abracadabra?"

"Uh-uh."

"Open the door, or I'll huff, and I'll puff and I'll . . ." and it went on like that until she said the password, which not even the neighbors or our best friends could know (nor could they know we were home alone or there'd be more trouble than all of us combined could talk our way out of Mom said, often and sternly).

When we were home alone, I liked to imagine myself a competent and crafty little mother. "Let's get our homework done so we can play a game," I'd say, unlocking our apartment door with a key so plain you'd never imagine the weight it carried. I'd plop apples and buttered Pilot Bread crackers on the table, and we'd bend our industrious little heads to reading and writing. Though I always stuffed my math homework back in my bag half-finished because I was guaranteed to get most of it wrong anyway. After that, we'd read or build forts or chase each other across the Chinese Checkers board. We had it pretty good for a pair of girls without a parent around.

One day I asked Tekla if she wanted to play checkers, and she slapped the checkerboard to the floor, kicked the marbles across the room, and burst into tears. She curled up on the floor pillows, crying so hard I worried the neighbors would call the cops. You might have thought someone had threatened her actual life, but I knew it for a hunger attack.

"I'll help you," I promised, trying to grab a flailing hand. "Just, *please*, tell me what you need." Tekla shook her head. "PB&J? Hot dog? Ramen?" Mom had a strict no-cooking rule when we were home alone. What if the kitchen caught fire, or we boiled each other alive for fun? Microwave only. But I felt myself running down blind roads of hysteria. "Macaroni and cheese?" She nodded, finally, cries softening as I ran to the kitchen.

I followed the directions on the cardboard box: boil water, add noodles, drain them. Then a splash of milk, butter, the cheese packet, and *voila!* Tekla sat at the table, silent tears watering her noodles while I climbed counters in search of the hidden box of graham crackers. When I couldn't find them in the usual hidey-holes, I set my sights on the small cupboards above the stove's hood, absently stepping on the stovetop to reach them.

I remember the sizzling sound the electric coils made when I stepped on the hot burner the way you remember, over and over, the last second before your head hits the steering wheel during a car wreck. I remember, too, the smell of burnt flesh blackening on the coil as I tore my foot free. I sat on the sink while Tekla ate, running cold water over my foot and licking tears from my top lip. I knew I would hide the burn. Mom would forbid me to cook again. I needed her to trust me more, not less, and we simply couldn't wait for her to come home to feed us anymore.

Outside of singing with Mr. Norman's choir and weekend cuddle puddles with Mom and Tekla, the only other thing I wanted in the world was Camden home with us. Instead, Thom brought me a bike. Not only was it pink (gag me) with glittery pink tassels (why?), it had white puffy clouds on the seat that caused me to wonder if Thom had forgotten just what kind of pink-hater I was in the two years since he left. But the bike had a banana seat, and that made up for its girlish failings in every way. The plain truth is that thing put a fear in me I couldn't name. I did not know how to ride a bike. Instinct told me I'd be the butt of every joke on the block if I didn't take secret nighttime lessons before I ever let one kid from the neighborhood set eyes on it. A neighbor kid was bound to beat me up and take it once they saw how weak I was.

I thanked Thom for the gift, dancing around in the street and hugging him over and over until he said, "Okay. Okay." But when I made to walk it down to our building, his eyebrows went up. "Hold on. Aren't you gonna take it for a test ride?" he said.

"I will!" I called over my shoulder, pushing the handles a little harder.

"Hey!" he shouted in that hoarse way he had of talking loud. He threw in a whistle to get my attention. "C'mere a minute."

I dreaded turning to face him. I did an exasperated shoulder slumping *please just let me get about my very important eight-year-old business* head roll as I turned back.

"Let's see it!" Thom said. I looked dead at his eyes, but what I actually saw was me on the pavement, buried under that ridiculous pink bike. I saw the big kids from across the street doubled over and drooling with laughter.

Thom squatted down in the street as I approached, white T-shirt straining against his chest as though it would make a bid for freedom if only it weren't so safely tucked into the waistband of those worn-out-but-still-good Levi's.

"Why don't you get on?" he said as I slowed on approach. When I still didn't answer, he said, even more gently, "You don't know how to ride yet?"

I shook my head, having learned ages before that it was better to stand mute in the face of Thom's disappointment than to break into tears. I had his whole speech memorized: "Punkin', emotions are a product of the brain that can get in the way of your ability to think. But since *you* are in control of your brain, you control your emotions. And when you control your emotions, you can think clearly during emotional situations."

The logic of this argument always caught me off guard. And it didn't change anything. Tears still regularly got the better of me anyway. Particularly where Thom was concerned. I couldn't believe he'd taken Camden and left us so completely. He'd moved to a whole *other town*. I didn't understand the choices Mom and he had made, and at that age, I couldn't have untangled the complicated feelings that went into their split if they'd told me outright. What I felt was betrayed.

I stood there looking at my not very long-lost stepdad while trying to avoid his dead-serious gaze.

"It's your lucky day, then," Thom said cheerfully. Absolutely the last thing you wanted to hear when emotions were already as thick and confused as taffy in your teeth.

I doubt any one of the Apostles could change Thom's mind once he'd made it up. You didn't say to him, *Now's no good, how about next week?* You didn't say, *Everyone's watching.* Or, *I made it this far without a bike.* He'd convinced Mom to marry him by persisting each and every time she said *no*. It hadn't exactly worked out the way he'd planned, but still, it worked.

I let Thom's determination carry me onto that banana seat and keep me there, slowly turning the pedals while he raised the kickstand. He gripped the seat as effortlessly and surely as Spock doing his Vulcan nerve pinch.

"Keep turning the pedals," Thom said. But even with his strong hands supporting the bike's frame, a wobble in the wheel shook right through my spine and left me feeling fragile as chipped china.

"Whoa," I said. "Can we take a break?"

He hit me with that sideways grin. I wanted to hate the faint smell of aftershave that clung to him, the crease in his knuckles. How could he just quit being my dad?

"Keema," Thom said, "I believe you are afraid of what you don't understand. What you need to know is that these two wheels"—he pointed at the bike's tires—"are at your mercy. As long as you steer them confidently with your handlebars, and you propel them with appropriate force, you will be in command of this vehicle." His face had the lumberjack's unapologetic serenity as he felled an entire forest tree by tree. "You have nothing to fear."

I wanted to tell him I couldn't remember a time in my life that I hadn't felt fear. I wanted to upend the bucket of tears I hid from him. The ones I habitually saved up until they spilled over at my classmate's birthday parties when they had particularly nice fathers. The kind of tears that made my friends ask, *Why are you crying?* To which I'd reply, *Because I don't have a dad*, and then I'd have to explain how I actually had two: but the first one didn't want me, and the other one let me go. I wanted to point out to Thom that as a second-grader, I knew nothing of confidence. The last thing I wanted was to be in command of a moving vehicle so naked to the world that a stick in the spokes might undo it.

I glared at him with badger eyes.

"You can't make me," I said. "You're not my dad anymore."

He coughed out a rough chuckle and said, "I'm right here, Punkin'. You just keep pedaling, and I'll just keep holding on."

I pedaled until he told me to pedal backward to brake, which I did. Five minutes later, he said, "Now you know how to ride a bike." And I did, even after he left town again.

Thom had brought Tekla a bike, too, and taught her to ride almost as easily as he taught me. "You're still my girls," he told us before he left. It was a directive. I wanted to say, *Then why don't you bring Camden and stay here?* But as a two-year veteran of this ex-husbands-and-wives thing, I already knew better than to ask.

Those bicycles gave us all kinds of freedom. We scouted for loose change in the parking lots and took our haul to a building down the way where an industrious couple had set up a kind of candy shop out of their apartment. They had a long list of tempting goodies tacked to their front door that were mostly out of our price range. We stuck with Rocky Roads and Oh Henry! bars for a quarter, or Tootsie Pops for a dime. We never managed to save up our loot for something special, like a Klondike Bar, which cost a dollar.

With bikes, we could play at the bigger, better-equipped playground on the other side of the neighborhood and still get home to check in every hour without spending most of our weekend playtime walking back and forth. We alternated checking in or played Ro Sham Bo to see who got to stay and play while the other rushed home. We didn't have a watch to go by, but some internal clock gave me a preternatural ability to gauge time if I wanted to.

"It's time to check-in," I'd say, and Tekla, twisted up on the swing set with her friends, would say, "Already? We just went."

At home, Mom would be busy with a book or an art project, and she'd say, "You're the best kids a girl could ask for." And then, "Check in again in an hour."

With a bike of my own, I had power and speed. I never won a neighborhood race with my short little legs, even pedaling full steam, but I didn't come in dead last, either. The athletic genes in the family went to Tekla. But I hadn't figured that out yet, so I barreled carelessly over curbsides and tree branches and off small jumps, regularly skidding across the pavement on hands and knees.

I ventured farther every day until, eventually, I braved the road leading out of our neighborhood toward a larger connecting road.

This, despite the fact that Mom had previously got her stern face on specifically to say, "I trust you to stay out of the road. Don't get yourself in trouble." Which I knew meant, *I trust you, but you're eight years old.* I didn't figure my age as an accurate assessment of my reliability, though. I already cooked and did dishes and kept track of time, not to mention watching my brother and sister all summer. For *free*, I might add.

The road was slick with those leftover gravelly bits that were laid down over the ice every winter but never swept away. I found this exhausting and exhilarating at once. I spent an inordinate amount of time racing up and down that stretch of road until one day, a car sped around the corner, surprising me. I braked so hard I left a black stain on the pavement as I launched into the ditch. I was staring up from the blueberry bushes before my brain caught up with the fact that I'd gone over the handlebars.

I was shocked to find I hadn't broken anything. I sat for a while, contemplating several hundred scratches that now decorated my arms and legs and a rock the size of a nickel buried in the skin above my left kneecap. This made for a painful walk home once I finally shook the ringing from my ears. Blood ran freely down my leg to stain my socks. I shed a disproportionate volume of tears over the situation as I gasped and spluttered and hobbled down the street.

I found my mother asleep on the living room floor in the pile of throw cushions. She lay on one side with a book splayed out beside her. The tin box she stashed her weed in sat open on the table. It held a jewel-colored glass pipe, rolling papers, and a lighter nestled atop a small plastic baggy inside. The box rarely sat where we could see it, but it wasn't a secret, either. "Everybody does it," she assured us. "Nobody talks about it. Especially not you kids. Not ever."

Mom woke slowly when I collapsed dramatically in front of her, as though surfacing from a deep lake. She took in my tears and the blood staining my socks with mild interest. I explained about the car and the gravelly road, and the blueberry bushes. She gave me a look that said, *What'd I tell you?*

She sighed.

"Use the tweezers in the medicine cabinet to pull the rocks," she said. "Make sure you wash out all the dirt."

What I needed was stitches. The little pebbles came out easy, but the larger one took every drop of willpower I had. It had gone so deep that pulling it free seemed about as possible as performing an appendectomy on myself. Finally, I gave up on slow and gentle and ripped the thing out like a bad tooth. One little piece broke free, and try as I might, I could not get those tweezers back in there. The pain was lightning against a black sky. I left it.

The wound eventually healed around the shattered bit of rock that remained. It left an irritated, red lump that migrated around my kneecap until it resurfaced years later so you could see the grey of it pressed against my taut skin. Eventually, it rose close enough to the surface that I cut it free with a razor blade. Now there's a wide scar where the rock went in, and another one a little north of that, where it exited somewhere around my eleventh birthday.

That night I lay in bed with a throbbing in my knee so fierce I wanted the whole leg cut right off. I wondered if my mother's gentle hands might have done a better job of it, but then it occurred to me I'd never have asked for her help. She'd done her part, telling me to keep out of the road. And I'd done mine. It doesn't get any more fair than that. I figured if I was old enough to ignore the rules, I was old enough to suffer the consequences.

It gave me an orphaned feeling, though.

I might have had more freedom than a lot of kids my age, but it wouldn't matter much if I used that freedom to get myself killed.

When I'd crawled out of that ditch and started limping home, I'd stopped to look back. I'd have been invisible from the road down in those blueberry bushes. The next person to drive by would have seen only an abandoned bike on the roadside: pink, with glittery pink tassels and clouds on the seat. Abandoned bikes were strewn all over Gruening Park. One more wouldn't turn any heads. You'd have had to know where to look to find me down there in the culvert among the fiddlehead ferns and berry bushes. That driver hadn't even stopped to check on me.

The best thing about running errands with Mom was the bag of Peanut M&M's at the checkout stand (her favorite, not mine, but candy all the same). But I dreaded it too. All that endless walking through aisles and aisles of food and the new clothes we couldn't even afford to look at.

Shopping became a game of hide-and-seek among the circular clothes racks in the home goods section or crawling into the shelves holding camping gear. We inevitably scattered like roaches before she'd finished saying, "Stay where I can see you."

One time she found me inside a rack of men's shirts and snatched me up off the floor so fast we knocked a pile of woolen plaids to the floor with a clatter of upset hangers.

"This is not a game," she hissed. "There are bad people in this world looking to steal little girls like you." Her voice ran a shaky line between fear and rage. She marched me to the dairy aisle and pointed out the pictures of missing children printed on the milk cartons. They were always such small children, hardly big enough to dress themselves. "Every single one of these kids is loved by someone. *Missed* by someone. Do you know what would happen to me if you were on this carton?" I shook my head. "I would never forgive myself," she said. I believed her.

Grandma Gorgeous Darling put in an endless bid for us all to move back to Ketchikan. "You need family," she argued. "You're just not safe in a big city like Juneau," which boasted a population of just over 25,000 compared to Ketchikan's 8,000.

Mom laughed it off. "Where there's a will, there's a way," she loved to say. "The world is only a scary place if you don't think you have to pay attention."

~

Mom called her boyfriends *suitors*. At twenty-eight, she had a lush figure, three kids by two different dads, and she still held big dreams about art school and music.

I didn't mind the boyfriends. They weren't exactly dinner guests. They typically visited only after we were in bed, and when we were up, they kept their hands to themselves. Occasionally Mom might say, "You don't need to mention Andy when Rob comes over later," which warmed my heart. More than one suitor meant none were serious.

Until one day, it changed.

I didn't know Mom had begun accepting applications for the job of dad number three. The stress of single parenting, work, and school had her on the verge of coming unglued, but I didn't recognize that. I saw only what I wanted to see: bedtime silliness; strong, soft hands; her paintings multiplying in the corner of the living room. So it knocked me out when she picked me up from school one day at the beginning of third grade and asked if I thought she should marry C.A.

I couldn't picture the man's face; that's how little I knew him, which wouldn't have mattered anyway. I wanted her to myself. I'd have rather given up singing than go through the dad thing again. Mom's smile, though—wide and hopeful and dreamy—gave me a sudden bout of carsickness. I said *yes* even though I felt the *no* burning in my throat. They were married from the following spring until the end of my eighth-grade year.

I don't recall how it happened that Mr. Norman took us Christmas shopping before we left Juneau. It didn't occur to me at the time to think it unusual that our school choir teacher felt the need to buy Tekla and me presents, except that a thin sliver of confusion followed the gifts home. Mom had been accepted into a BFA program at the University of Alaska, Fairbanks, and we were already packed for a dead-of-winter move. So maybe they were more like going away presents.

"Pick anything you want," Mr. Norman urged us. I wondered if he had kids of his own to shop for, but I never got up the courage to ask. "Something fun," he said.

We walked the tiny Gold Nugget Mall, and he pointed out a tape player, a Glo Worm, a tie-dye kit. All seriously fun things I would have killed for. But our footwear situation had become desperate, and we settled on snow boots. Striped rainbow boots with inch-thick padding stuffed into a thin nylon shell that drew together with a string at the top. I sighed. I'd have been way more excited about the tape player.

"I've never taught anyone like you girls before," Mr. Norman told us later, over pizza. "You are a little grown-up," he said to me. "And you are an absolute songbird," he said to Tekla, unwittingly defining our life's trajectories.

"It's not enough though, is it?" I asked.

Mr. Norman nodded sadly as though he understood the exact shape and size of my many worries. I wasn't ready to try out another dad. I wasn't ready to give up my weekends playing Chinese checkers and card games whenever we wanted or the classmates I finally knew by name.

"Even a very responsible child can't take the place of another adult in the house," he said eventually. I wished we hadn't started choir extra early, special as it might be. Now I had a thing to miss. And a person. I felt like I had enough to worry over already.

I wished he had applied for the open stepdad position.

What kind of *peapod* would we be with Camden in Sitka at Thom's while Tekla and I were stuck out on an icefield with Mom and this new guy? We'd barely got our routine down without Camden, and now we had to make room for a perfect stranger. Gone were the morning cuddle puddles, books in bed, me sipping off Mom's hot coffee, and eating cereal for at least two meals. They weren't even married yet, and already I felt her slipping away. How would C.A. fit into our summers of music festivals?

It made me sleepy.

We sat quietly with Mr. Norman, watching snow pile up in the parking lot through the mall's wide glass doors. Great wet flakes drifted careless and wind-drunk through the dark sky. They piled up on evergreen branches and telephone poles as readily as the warm hood of a running engine, where they melted and ran to the pavement, indifferent to their changing form. I ached to care so little for where the wind might take me next.

Cold Ground

~~~

I hesitate to call the smile on Mom's face a happy one when we pulled into Fairbanks. There seemed to be a lot of worry under it—a pile of unasked questions. C.A. had a bootlegged recording of the Grateful Dead running on the tape cassette player and the defrost blowing full steam on the icy windshield. Tekla and I were two buckets of tears in the back seat, staring in misery at the walls of snow plowed several cars deep alongside the highway. We'd made the move just before the new year to give us all time to unpack before classes started.

Great. All that frozen white winter to play in, snow like I'd never seen before, and not one friend to share it with except my sister. Misery laid on me as heavy and fixed as a great invisible house cat with its claws dug in. It sucked all generosity of spirit right out of me.

As far as I could tell, the only thing Fairbanks had going for it was its proximity to the North Pole. Which I discovered, to my surprise, is a town. I thought this meant that Fairbanks was about as far north as you could go, a fact I shared with the pen-pal assigned to me at school who lived someplace that seemed tropical and foreign to my mind. Georgia, I think. When I eventually learned that North Pole (the town) is not, in fact, the point in the

Northern Hemisphere where the Earth's axis of rotation meets its surface, I accepted this as proof of the Alaska school system's failure to equip me with a sufficient grasp of geography. Somehow, the disconnect between Alaska and the rest of the continental United States always left me feeling like the rest of America was a myth.

The mid-winter move had found me only loosely equipped for serious weather. The mild, slushy snows of the Southeast hadn't prepared me for the bitter, biting, finger and toe-eating *cold* of Interior Alaska. I stepped out of the car on that first day in a hoodie and jeans and felt my neck muscles seize all the way up to my eyebrows.

"Are you kidding me!?" I shouted into a careless grey sky. I looked back at Tekla, hunched under a blanket in the back seat and glaring out the open door. I sighed and rolled my eyes in agreement. Gone were the days of raincoats over sweaters or lightly lined cotton and denim coats in December.

We learned to dress in layers for the briefest outings: cotton, wool, down, scarf, hat, mittens. I soon realized that layers meant despair if I forgot to hit the bathroom before racing out the door to catch the bus in the morning. The forty-five-minute ride to school inevitably found me fighting my way out of all that gear in the tiny bathroom at Joy Elementary. I occasionally didn't make it in time.

Much of Alaska huddled indoors that January, necks tucked firmly under wings, collectively warding off the chill of a powerful cold spell. Juneau's average low hovered right at three below, but Fairbanks trended toward climate extremes like I hadn't seen before. I didn't much care for it. When the thermostat dropped to sixty below a few weeks after our move, I declared myself homesick for the wet winters of Juneau and vowed to get out of Fairbanks as fast as I could. By then, I'd already been curled up listlessly in bed with Nancy Drew for days on end. Mom's student budget didn't have room for indoor fun, like movies or roller-skating rinks, or video arcades. Bed seemed the safest place to pass the time.

Mom finally came in, rolling her eyes. "It's not all bad," she said, ducking down to crawl into the bottom bunk with me.

That was fine for her to say. She always got to decide where we lived, how long we stayed, what we did there. She didn't have to start over as the new kid again, sporting ratty thrift-store clothes and a weird name. I mean, she did, but I felt like college might be friendlier for grown-up weirdos than elementary school was for kid weirdos. It never took her more than five minutes to drum up a couple of musicians, and she'd be off in a jam session, lost in a cloud of pot smoke and home-brewed beers.

I huffed, kicked at my blankets, and threw my book on the floor. Our first Fairbanks apartment may have surpassed 600 square feet, but not the way I remember it. I felt like a betta fish with too much competition in a too-small bowl. I whined about the cold, turned my nose up at grilled cheese sandwiches, and generally complained about everything. Inside: boredom paralyzed you. Outside: snow piled up on the swing sets, and brittle air froze the snot in your nose on the first breath.

"You have to find ways to make fun here, or the cabin fever will kill you," Mom said. "Even if frostbite doesn't." She kindly refrained from suggesting that if neither of them succeeded, she might be forced to finish the job herself unless I got my act together.

"It's not like I left you kids to fend for yourselves out on some abandoned homestead an hour from town," she pointed out. I knew plenty about that particular part of her story. I knew what life on the homestead had been like for her. I knew enough about her brother in the dark rooms and the brass knuckles he used to keep her silent to understand the difference between our worlds. I knew she'd run away from it all and had us kids to save her sanity.

I knew it, and still I said, "Yeah, but you made us leave everyone we know so you could go to school. And now we have no friends, and we can't afford to go anywhere, and it's too cold to play outside. You might as well have left us on an iceberg." It hurt to be such a low priority that she'd added C.A. to the mix in the first place. Then she'd gone and hauled us off to this frozen hell and stuffed us in a cold bunk bed while she disappeared for school all hours of the day.

I ached at the tears standing in her eyes even as I blistered her with my misery.

"I'm not bored," I whispered. "I'm lonely." I wiped my nose on the sleeve of my sweater. "I miss you."

Mom stared at the wooden slats of the upper bunk as if hoping to find a shred of grace up there.

"I'm doing the best I can," she said on a slow breath. "School is so important. It's going to help me take better care of you." She ran a hand over her eyes, pressing back those unshed tears. "No one else in our family has a college degree. Did you know that?"

I nodded as though I understood already that this was the new normal and she'd be in school until I was well out of the house. I'd heard her on the phone with the university a few days earlier, trying to sort through all her years of credits at so many different colleges. Her frustration at having to repeat courses. "I'm just trying to make something good come of all this hard work," she'd sighed into the phone.

"It's important," I said, diving into her arms. "I know. It's important." I swallowed back the part of me that trembled and sobbed for want of being so important that I could come first for a change.

We laid there quietly for long minutes, staring up at the scarred underside of the used bunk bed. Her arms warmed me better than ten thousand blankets.

"Have you ever seen hot coffee freeze in the air?" Mom asked, offhandedly.

I shrugged, snuffling.

"I hear it freezes solid," she said. "Should we try it?"

Of course, I said *yes*. You had to take every opportunity for silliness that popped up with a mother as busy as mine.

She brewed a fresh cup of coffee while I sorted through unpacked boxes in search of thick socks and a scarf to wind around my nose. C.A. sat on the small thrift-store sofa in our tiny living room, maybe five feet by seven, watching a taped Cubs game.

"Seems like a waste of a good cup of coffee," he said when we told him our plan. This from the guy watching taped summer sports in January.

My soon-to-be-stepdad had me stumped. C.A. wore suspenders over checkered flannels, a scruffy black beard, and round Jerry Garcia glasses perched on his hooked nose. He liked beer, the Chicago Cubs, the Grateful Dead, and my mother, in equal measure. He worked as a carpenter and hosted a radio show on KTOO when we lived in Juneau for four of the six years we were together—not counting the summers we spent in Ketchikan or bouncing between folk festivals. As a person, I liked him all right. As a stepdad, I had mixed feelings. I liked that he loved my mother. But I still hated that I'd had to give up Thom in the first place, and now Mom spent more time with C.A. than she did with me. I wasted a lot of jealous energy making sure he knew my heart was a hard little nut he'd never crack.

"Dinner's on, girls," he'd say, having spent an hour chopping salad (yuck), sautéing vegetables (gross), and browning meat (even grosser). Then I'd sulk to the table, eat three bites, and glare at my plate until everyone finished, and I got invited to do the dishes in appreciation of my attitude.

In all fairness, it was going to be a hard deal for anyone who came along after Thom. He was a hard act to follow with his calm voice and surprise bedtime milkshakes, his penchant for wrestling on the living room floor after watching Kung Fu movies. And the fact that, from the very beginning, he'd never wasted an opportunity to brag that Tekla and I were his girls. Thom hadn't pretended to be anything but a kid at heart when he was with us. He loved go-karts and water parks and daredevil rides that made you puke. I tended to remember him as special and perfect. Until I recalled the part where he left us.

If everyone leaves in the end, what's the point in trying to figure them out?

Also, I couldn't quite understand why C.A. liked to scare the bejesus out of the dishes first thing in the morning. This had altered the sound of our early hours in an alarming way. He'd be up so early they hadn't decided what the day's news would be in Alaska yet. So he blasted Morning Edition on NPR while threatening anything hapless enough to lie about in the drying rack. Plus the coffee pot, the frying pan, and whatever instruments came to hand during the lunch-making process. If a particular piece of Tupperware displeased him—perhaps I hadn't washed every millimeter of it exactly perfectly, or drops of water rolled off the lid when he lifted it from the rack—it went sailing back into the pile of clean dishes like a fifteen-pound bowling ball. This was usually accompanied by a string of loud curses. *WHAT THE . . . ?! YOU GOTTA BE KIDDING ME!* Hangover talk, I'd learn.

It's possible C.A.'s fits didn't bother anyone else, but we were only a couple months into living with him, and they had me afraid to get out of bed in the mornings lest he turn on me. I learned to read which way the rooster spun before I dared say a thing. If he was humming, I'd eat a bowl of cereal at the table. If he was cussing at Bob Edwards on the radio, I snuck into the bathroom on whisper feet. The trick, I found, was to keep my mouth shut in the morning and only ask C.A. for things in the afternoon: after the second beer but before the fifth. Otherwise, if I wanted to go outside to play during a warm spell, it was hard to predict who would answer: giddy C.A. or surly stepdad. *Sure, is your homework done?* he might say one day, or *No,* and maybe, *Because I said so,* on another.

On this occasion, it pointed toward thinking that throwing a cup of coffee in the air was a silly thing to do. Which I can't say is entirely wrong.

Heat gushed through the front door as we stepped outside, rising with such force toward the pale stars blinking icily above us you'd think we'd unleashed a vent direct from the Earth's core.

"Holy cccccow," I said, neck instantly seized up with shivers.

"I would use stronger words," Mom said, tossing the steaming cup upwards. The coffee instantly dispersed into a cloud of crystals so fine she might have thrown up powdered chocolate. We gasped. The crystals hung there, drifting like so much mist on a bitter breeze before trailing to the crusty snow on our front stoop.

Cool, I wanted to say.

I still miss you, I wanted to say.

But every drop of moisture in my throat had turned to dust.

Dark winter mornings in Fairbanks found Tekla and me shouldered up against each other like misplaced penguins, lost in the vapor of our own breath. The world beyond our unmarked bus stop loomed eerily out of the shadows cast by distant streetlamps. Snow and ice fog muffled the sound of traffic several blocks over. My daydreams alternated between the heater in Mom's yellow station wagon and the heavy blankets on our bunk beds. I liked to imagine the heat of my body snuggled down like a ghost in the nest I'd left.

On the coldest mornings, we tugged hats over our faces and tucked them into our coat collars, breathing shallowly to avoid soaking the material. I counted myself lucky to have Tekla to lean on, unlike those poor kids without siblings or the ones who shared stops with random neighbors. We shivered blindly in place, listening for the soft clink of chained bus tires beyond the intermittent squeal and hiss of frozen brakes on the train tracks a block away. I tallied each train that passed, promising myself I'd be back in the balmy rainforests where I belonged before I counted to three hundred. I never remembered the tally from one counting to the next, so I'm left with a best guess, but I suppose it has to be near a thousand.

During our second winter in Fairbanks, Camden joined us at the bus stop across the street from our new house, just off College Road. He followed us out in his pajamas to wait with Tekla and me, despite my objections.

"It's too cold," I said, pushing him back inside. The average monthly temperature in December that year hovered around six below. Not nearly as cold as the January before, but cold enough. "Watch us from the window," I told him. "We'll wave to you before we go."

Winter visits with Camden were only as long as Christmas break, and two weeks felt like too little time to catch up on the months apart. Whenever we three were together, we functioned like a many-headed monster. Everybody knows it's hard to separate a many-headed monster, especially with Christmas on the horizon. Despite my objections, he dragged a jacket over his pajamas, stomped into a pair of galoshes, and followed us to the corner. We skate-scooted on our shoes in the icy road, climbed the eight-foot snow berm at the side of the street to play King-of-the-Hill, and kicked loose gravel at random targets for points.

By the time our bus rumbled to the corner, we'd worked up a sweat. Tekla and I waved at Camden through the windows, aiming air kisses at his pink face. He laughed, coppery hair spiked with exertion and ran alongside the bus. Soon he'd grown small as a piece of road gravel behind us. Then he disappeared, leaving a quiet flutter in my chest.

It would be hours before the first blush of sunrise laid a promise of gold and rose upon our heavily tracked snow berm.

Imagine Camden's surprise when he skate-scooted home in the dark, looking forward to a bowl of cereal and maybe some Lego time in front of our tiny black-and-white television, only to find himself stuck in the arctic entry and locked out of the main house.

Arctic entryways are common in Alaska. They're small, unheated, closet-sized entry rooms for storing snowy boots and wet gear. They feature a door from the outside at one end and a door to the main house on the other. Most people only bothered to lock the inside door because it's a hassle to find your keys with mittens on. With the outer door closed, Camden was protected from the wind, but that's about it.

Mom didn't do mornings with us anymore. Tekla and I usually made our own breakfasts and lunches now, only waking her in case of emergency: for loose change if we were low on food in the house and needed lunch money or an occasional ride to school when we missed the bus. She had her hands full with school, and art shows to prepare for. We knew to let her sleep. But Camden never could sleep late. Most days, he still woke between four and five and then spent ten minutes flipping the lights on and off, trying to wake Tekla and me so we'd play with him.

Mom, still asleep in her bedroom at the back of our small house, couldn't hear the pounding of Camden's little fists on the door. I doubt it was more than a few minutes before some small part of her noticed the quiet in the house after we left. Even in slumber, her mother's brain knew the absence of war cries and nuclear explosions and boyish mayhem beyond her chamber door meant one of two things: Camden was either sick in bed, or he was up to something.

Eventually, the silence roused her. She wandered through the house calling for him. She'd searched every nook, cupboard, and cranny before pausing to peer out the window. There she caught a faint, kittenish mewl from the front door. Inside the arctic entry, she found her small son huddled in a pile of coats, arms tucked into his jacket, lips blue, tears frozen to cheeks and lashes.

"Even half an hour can kill a person up here," Mom said when Tekla and I got home from school, the tremor in her voice one I recognized as, *Get out of the road, don't you see the car coming?* She pointed out the window. "That's not rain falling from the sky," she said. "It's snow." She grabbed my shoulder for extra emphasis.

"I can't even fathom what you were thinking," she said. I stared at my socks, wet from snow spilling over my boot tops to melt around my ankles. I recalled our coffee experiment from the year before. It wasn't nearly as cold as back then, but it gave me shivers anyway, imagining Camden's small body exploding into an icy mist.

I'm sorry, I wanted to say.

I want to go home, I wanted to say.

But every drop of moisture in my throat had turned to dust.

Dome Sweet Dome

~~~

Sometime after our move to Fairbanks, I began to have a recurring dream that I still have to this day when I'm stressed.

I walk for hours through the giant maze of a dream mansion, searching for a room of my own. I am heartsore and lonesome. Every room is occupied. Every closet, bathtub, or cupboard is claimed. No matter how the shape of the house changes—the location, the size, or the number of rooms—I search for hours before finding the perfect place. Usually, it is a secret place, buried so deep in the house that surely no one could know about it or even want it. *I can live here!* I think, finding a box behind a water heater. Finally, a place of my *own*.

Always, I am told that space is reserved for someone else. Look elsewhere.

In recent years, sleep labs have discovered that dreaming occurs in real-time. I suppose this means I've spent several thousand hours, maybe more, looking for a place to call my own. In all my dreams, I never once landed one.

Maybe it started with the homeless dreams, but during our first frozen winter in Fairbanks, the idea of living in a snow cave implanted itself in my mind so ferociously that it overwhelmed my every waking moment. I imagined the freedom of a place of my own right next door to Mom. I'd sleep in a nest of down warmed by my own breath, with the wind and the wild stars to hold me. Plus, I could run an extension cord to my place for a tiny space heater as long as the cold temperatures held. And if hunger knocked, I could slip inside for hot chocolate and leftovers whenever I liked.

I figured there were less feasible childhood ambitions, like growing up to be a vet. Which, in fact, I'd wanted very much to do until some kind soul pointed out I'd have to stitch bloody gashes, poke needles at critters with claws on four appendages, and euthanize dogs and cats. Living in a house made of snow, by comparison, seemed like a thing a serious person could actually *do*.

Opportunity struck in February when the city plowed ten feet of neighborhood snow into our driveway three days running. They worked so vigilantly that the sound of the plows scraping ice beneath our window became a new normal.

On Saturday morning, Tekla and I suited up and exhausted ourselves packing down the pile of snow with our sleds and boots before setting to work tunneling into the massive heap with our hands. We dug a foot of girl-sized tunnel that way but were eventually forced to stomp into the house in search of better digging tools and dry gloves. Half an hour later, we returned with empty coffee cans and a plan: we would build a cozy home just for us.

We scooped snow with our coffee can pails past nightfall, which isn't saying much when the sun sets as early as 4 p.m. in February. The entrance sloped downward, a frozen gopher hole that led to a chamber large enough for Tekla and me to sit in comfortably. We celebrated with twenty-five-cent kid cones at the Hot Licks ice cream parlor across the street. We were so cold the ice cream felt warm on our tongues. By Sunday afternoon, we'd dug two smaller sleeping rooms at either side of the living room and were ready to drag our bedding outside. Mom put the kibosh on that after poking her head in to check on us.

"You girls sure know how to think big," she'd said at first, which we thought sounded like approval. We had built a small home of *snow*, using *coffee cans*. Weren't we the most industrious eight and nine-year-old girls in the world? Mom didn't fit through the tunnel well enough to cozy up in the living room with us, but we proudly showed her each of our new bedrooms.

"That's mine," Tekla said, claiming the room to the right.

"That's mine," I said, pointing left. "And we're moving out here tonight!"

"Yeah . . . I don't think so." Mom said, genuine sorrow turning the corners of her mouth down. "For so many reasons." Freezing temps, warming temps, collapse, predators; they were all good reasons. But still. The end of a childhood fantasy is no less heartbreaking because of its impracticality.

Our lopsided structure stood there for months. Waiting. Useless. Snow filled our footprints and drifted through the tunnel door. I couldn't bring myself to play in it again.

At night I imagined a pack of wolves dragging a carcass into the cozy central room or bearing litters in my sleeping nook. By day I could hardly stand the sight of it. It was just another house that could never be my home. I wished for spring to come and ease my longing.

Instead, spring came and delivered a giant Plexiglas dome. Mom won the kit from a call-in radio contest. I'd worked for days to build my snow house, but Mom won the dome with a single, well-timed phone call. C.A. hammered the kit out, cursing now and then over the odd piece, but it came together in no time. Soon we had a shimmery new room in the backyard, big enough for C.A. to stand in. The dome had probably been designed as a greenhouse, but Mom moved her art projects outside as spreading pools of water announced the end of the snow home I had shaped with my own two hands.

~

Summers in Fairbanks hit with such intensity it felt like the work of an evil professor with a grudge against winter. "We've been betrayed!" I told Tekla when my favorite sledding ditch melted into a thick slough and began churning out mosquitoes by the thousands. I'd been sledding down that massive culvert on an old garbage bag for months. It worried me that I'd been carelessly flinging my body onto a pile of snow perched atop a hidden body of water, sluggish and slow as it was. What if I'd punched through? I didn't like to think the only thing between me and drowning in a frigid stream that winter had been a thin layer of ice under all that deceptive snow.

You wouldn't expect such heat in a place like Fairbanks if you first saw it in January. By June of my first summer, I couldn't remember what it felt like to shiver beneath three or four hundred blankets. I had bigger problems. Like the galaxy of mosquito bites that had blossomed across my entire body.

"Are they bigger here?" I moaned, scratching my legs bloody. "Or are there just more of them?" Even the magic X—whereby you dig your thumbnail into the center of each bite in a half-agonizing, half-soothing cross pattern—didn't work on those bites.

"Both," C.A. said, tossing me a can of something that had to be one hundred percent DEET.

At first, Mom tried to lather us up with homeopathic bug dope. "Smell it! It's delicious!" she said. "Look, it's got peppermint and lavender and calendula. And it feels good on your skin."

"Sounds like some real nice lotion," we said, watching her rub it in while we slathered on the DEET. A week later, Mom's arms were one giant blister of mosquito bites in various stages of ooze, pucker, and peel.

"Well, shit." Mom said. "This stuff is for people who live in places where the mosquitoes aren't as big as airplanes." And that was it for the hippie sauce.

The mosquitoes couldn't stop me, though. I had a winter's worth of cabin fever stockpiled, and I could not have forced myself to stay indoors even if a tragic tropical disease like malaria had been at stake.

Tekla and I scavenged walking sticks from the woods and stalked imaginary prey through Creamer's Field, a vast stretch of marshland that had been donated to the state by an old-timey dairy family and set aside as a bird sanctuary. We chased squirrels, cawed after ravens, and ran away from moose with their horse faces and knobby-kneed calves.

Once, after a slow afternoon catching wood frogs in the marsh, we emerged from the weeds with more mosquito bites than freckles. Tekla pulled one long sleeve up to reveal an arm entirely welted over with bites. "I can't believe they can get through our clothes," she said, disgusted.

We swatted at the swarm as it tried to follow us home. "Still better than frostbite!" I said, and we made a run for it.

We were all squirrelly with homesickness by then. Mom called her musician friends back home in Juneau, getting a vicarious thrill from their summer festival plans. Tekla fell onto an endless stack of library books. I myself didn't know what to look forward to without the promise of ferrying between festivals and family in Ketchikan, Sitka, and Juneau. I decided not to look forward to anything at all.

We were a mopey bunch until Mom heard through the grapevine that a whole stream of summer music festivals ran from Fairbanks on south to Anchorage and beyond. "There's probably one every weekend!" she told us. We were just as wide-eyed and giggly about it as most kids get over the prospect of Disneyland.

We were several festivals in before Mom got the idea to hit up local vendors and offer to run a booth for them, which is how we wound up in Haines at the Southeast Alaska State Fair for the first time.

C.A. had boxed up the dome for the two-day drive. To reach Haines from the Interior, you have to cross into and back out of Canada. Mom found it necessary to remind us repeatedly not to joke about being kidnapped when the Mounties asked if we were hers, or she'd go ahead and give us away at her earliest convenience.

At the border, the Mounties asked, "Is this your mother?" and they must've seen the sweat on my upper lip, the strain behind my smile that was my best effort at behaving myself. They asked four more times. This was nothing compared to the grief they gave my mother over the Alpaca sweaters, for which they expected her to pay an import tax. Mom didn't get teary-eyed over much, but the Mounties caught her off guard.

"I'm taking them to Haines to *make* enough money to *get* there!" she told them with a jagged edge to her voice that said, *I'm doing everything I can here, boys. Help me out.*

It was enough. They sewed the bags shut and insisted that she have them checked as we crossed back into Alaska.

"This is what it feels like to be imprisoned in your own state," Mom groused, but I figured it as the price you paid to live somewhere so gorgeous and disconnected from everything that you could hardly believe it was related to the rest of the continent in the first place.

Driving south from Fairbanks into the wet warmth of Haines that first time felt like coming home to a hot shower and a warm meal after frostnip got your fingers and toes. I was a child of the rainforest. I'd never known such blistering cold or staggering heat as we got in Fairbanks. I couldn't even think on how much I'd missed the thin prick of rain on my bare arms and the rich breath of wet spruce until it came back to me in a lungful as we pulled up to the fairground.

C.A. set up the dome near an old barn, as far away from the main stage as possible so it could serve as a booth and campsite in one. Mom's sweaters and jewelry were stacked neatly on tables draped in a black cloth that also served as a privacy curtain for the sleep nest Tekla and I built in the space below. Mom and C.A. camped deeper in, keeping company with the boxes of wares and the food and beer coolers. In my dreams, now, I began searching through endless fields of dome houses made of glass. Frost clung to the joints between panes, burning my hands as I pounded on each building, begging for a place to stay. Every night I tore myself loose from those frantic lost-girl dreams with a panic so real it gave me shivers. I'd lay as still and tense as a fly just before you swat it, counting Tekla's soft breaths until my heart slowed. This made our nights there both creepy and familiar.

Mom had a new music buddy from Fairbanks, Maureen, who came down to play a set with her. They called themselves The Sophisticated Ladies and played old-timey jazz numbers up on the big stage in funky pillbox hats and clunky costume jewelry, occasionally filling in as MCs when the need arose. Everywhere they went, people seemed to know them and want them near at hand for the next set, or a jam session some few campsites over, or just to introduce them to another passel of musicians. By the time we left a week later, it felt like we had a whole new family in Haines.

"This was a *good* festival," Mom declared as we aimed the car towards the Canadian border. "Let's do it again."

"Let's do it *every* year," I said.

I don't remember if C.A. enjoyed it as much as we did.

We smiled at a new batch of Mounties at the border like we knew what we were doing. They only asked me once if I belonged to my mother because right away I told them I did and not to be asking any more stupid questions.

Some kind of festival magic carried us home. It lingered for a few weeks, even as the birch trees began to drop their bright, brittle leaves. Mom bought us new winter coats with the leftover money she'd made in Haines, forking over the cash with a smile.

"Where there's a will, there's a way," she said. Grateful-like, but with a touch of smug. And it's true. No matter where we lived, she had a way of making things happen you wouldn't believe possible.

Hold Still, Hold Still

~~~

The dome didn't survive a single season as an art studio. Wet weather hit that fall, and new paintings refused to dry while fresh canvasses threatened mold. Mom rented studio space in a tall apartment building downtown that was too derelict to rent to actual live-in tenants. The place was so clearly haunted I tried never to blink for fear of a ghost finding me desirable.

For a while, I dragged my cello to the studio after school, lugging it several floors up to Mom's room to practice while she painted and Tekla did her homework. Mom put the kibosh on our visits after she found us bouncing around in a pile of discarded fiberglass insulation in one of the empty apartments. "Ho-lee-shit," she said, in that slow way people do when they're too stunned to come up with actual words.

That night my cold bath ran pink with blood. "Why don't people *tell* you about things like fiberglass?" I yelled at the bathroom door, already knowing I'd receive no answer.

Mom employed us kids as her own personal muses in Fairbanks, just as she had in Juneau and Sitka and Ketchikan and Petersburg. We'd posed in gardens for watercolors, as wood sprites in the gnarled roots of old-growth trees and tall grasses, on rocky beaches for quick pencil sketches. We were lost children found over and over again by a shift in light and perspective or the quick-snap of the shutter as our mother's eye wandered the world beyond the lens of her camera.

During our second summer in Fairbanks, Mom cast us girls as the Three Graces for a major project. Camden won the lottery with his role as the Divine Fool, which sounded way cooler than being a Grace. I saw it as further proof that even as fools, boys seemed to always get the more exciting end of the stick.

Mom coated us all in plaster of Paris and glue, then bade us to stand still in the backyard until it dried. She generously poked air holes in the general vicinity of our nostrils before wandering off to make herself a cup of coffee. If I'd known ahead of time what the job entailed, I'd have faked a stomach bug. After a few minutes in that wet coffin, I doubted my chances of survival. One did not so much *breathe* through the useless air holes as meditate on how good it would feel if you *could* breathe.

Time passed at a speed only stillness can yield as the summer sun beat down on us in our shells. I practiced Darth Vader breathing until I saw stars and gave it up. I laughed at the mosquitoes drawn by our breath, hurling themselves against the plaster in vain. Then I tried to count the nearby birds by their calls but couldn't keep track because they flitted around constantly. So mindless. So free. Their un-plastered wings and their nostrils so unrestricted I almost hated them.

Listening to my own stuttery snorts and sniffs inside that slowly hardening cocoon about drove me crazy enough to break out of the plaster shouting, "Oh, yeah!" like Kool-Aid man. I set to work plotting out how I'd use my plaster cast doppelganger. A layer of flesh-colored paint, some orangey-red for the hair, jeans, and a T-shirt from the thrift store: Voila! A little me I could send off to school with Tekla while I got myself a day job, the better to afford the junk food and new clothes I thought would probably change my life. I could plant a huge garden and set my plaster twin to scarecrowing or prop her up at C.A.'s side of the bed while he slept. She'd scare the bejesus out of him when he woke for a midnight pee. Maybe he'd finally give up and leave us to enjoy having our mother to ourselves again.

Then, because I was feeling regretful for my smallness and C.A. wasn't a bad guy, I hoped he'd be happier without us than he seemed to be with us.

Eventually, my arms fell asleep in their frozen upright position, and I vowed never to let my mother trick me into another art project again.

I tried to guess at how many hours of my life I'd spent sitting unnaturally still while she painted and penciled and shaded portraits of me. It happened anywhere. Anytime. I'd be sitting on the couch with a book in my hand, and she'd get this look on her face. I didn't even have to see it. I felt it. Then she'd reach for the nearest sketchpad, saying, *Hold still, hold still.* I usually did so without complaint, at least until my neck seized up and I couldn't stand it anymore.

Better not to move, though. If I so much as scratched my nose—which became an irresistible temptation the very nanosecond a *Hold still* command was issued—and if I didn't re-situate myself in precisely the same posture as before, she'd sing out, *You moooooved.* Then we'd spend ten minutes tilting my head up, down, left, right, a little over here, too far, almost . . . there—an eye roll generating pastime if ever there was one.

By the time Mom cracked our plaster shells, I felt like a half-boiled crab with just enough juice left to wave my claws around in empty threat. I couldn't say if we'd been in there for twenty minutes or ten hours. Even the incessant battering of bloodthirsty mosquitos against my sweaty arms felt better than the sticky closeness of the plaster. Lucky me, though. Tekla got to plaster up twice for the third Grace.

Before we moved to Fairbanks, my mother's art had trended toward landscapes and portraits. Boats in the harbor. Mountains against a grey sky. My babysitter leaning against a wall. But her professors at UAF *tsk-tsked* what they called a lack of imagination, completely forgetting the great Alaska tradition of bold landscapes. *Symbolism*, they told her. *You will work with symbolism if you wish to graduate from our program.*

At home, she said, "This isn't what I came here to do!" But on campus, she bent to her work willingly enough. Which is how her thesis project came to be a study she described as "the divine balance between masculine and feminine, as seen through the lens of the Star of David and interpreted by the tarot."

Symbolism lingers in her work today, but in my estimation, her best pieces recall the landscapes of her childhood. Fishermen at work. Rocky beaches. Quiet islands with their storied people and wandering waterways. Those are the tales her hands itch to tell—the places she brings to life. They're the stories she raised me in, the places we always returned to even as we grew up and apart.

The Three Graces were lifelike too, in a way that made my heart ache. I forgot all about the misery of the wet plaster when I saw the figures mounted at Mom's thesis show in the campus gallery just before Christmas. Only when my mother stood beside them, chatting with one of her professors, did I realize how small they were next to her five-foot-three frame.

I had to remind myself those three small figures were us: Tekla, Camden, and me. Tekla's had two inches on mine, but still. You couldn't tell the models were redheads, or that the clothes we'd worn were threadbare. They held hands and laughed eternally, never to dream or yearn or weep for want of a home. They danced around an imaginary maypole with arms raised in celebration right there in the middle of a hushed reception room while Camden's Divine Fool looked on. Our avatars stood in a circle like mummified sprites. Solid as cement; pale as apparitions.

Three tiny children. So very small, and yet they seemed to know more about everything than I could ever hope to learn. They knew every minute where they belonged in the world. In that way, they seemed more real than I had ever been. I envied them. They were born of my mother as much as me, but they would never miss her, need her, or resent the things that took her from them. They were free to simply exist.

In a few weeks, we were to leave for Ketchikan, just in time to do Christmas the way only Grandma Gorgeous Darling could do Christmas: millions of twinkle lights, porcelain angels, fine china at the table. No fooling around in the kitchen while scrubbing dishes. We'd enroll in school there for a month or two before ferrying over to Juneau. By then, Mom would have found a place for us to live, and we'd return to Harborview Elementary to finish out the spring of fifth grade. In time our years in Fairbanks would dim to the collective half-remembered nostalgia reserved for awkward family vacations.

Those Graces followed us, though. Years later, I'd stumble on them huddled in a storage room or stored in someone's basement with other things of ours. They seemed oddly content with patiently waiting for us to figure out a place to stay for a long stretch. I'd sometimes stand between my sister's Grace and my brother's fool and spread my arms to join their eternal dance, marveling at their guileless pleasure. Their slight frames, the way they seemed always to reach for each other, even when placed far apart. My sleeping self could never find a place to call home, but these figures had no such trouble. Wherever we went, there they were: unbreakable in their plaster of Paris. I only ever floated like a dream between places.

The Way of the Boothie

~~~

I jogged toward the coffee stand, rubbing the quarters Mom had given me between my fingers, awed by their slight weight and the way they warmed in my palm. So small, taken individually. But when you added them up, they could transform into pop and a cheeseburger, maybe even a milkshake. I so rarely had the occasion to carry money around that I wished for the power to replicate them, to turn this coffee refill mission into a warm belly and a neon pink fanny pack.

The guy at the fish n' chips booth leaned out of his order window as I raced by, and I casually swerved away as if I hadn't seen him. "Hey, kid!" he called.

I spun a quick circle, hoping to find someone else behind me.

Shoot.

I turned to the guy, wary as a long-tail vole. I'd snatched a handful of his tiny condiment packets that morning to liven up our plain hot dogs—ketchup, mustard, mayo. Plain hot dogs are *so* hard to choke down. I wondered if he could get me kicked out of the festival for that.

I stared up at him for three hundred years before finally raising a finger to point at myself. *Who, me?*

"You're at the sweater booth, right?" he asked, knocking a napkin loose from a stack as he leaned an elbow on the window ledge.

Double shoot. How did he know me already?

I groaned softly, wishing I could lie but knowing already that my scorched cheeks would give me away faster than Pinocchio's nose if I tried.

I nodded reluctantly.

"See if your mom wants to do a trade," he said. "A family size fish n' chips each day for one of those sweaters."

I stared at him for another three hundred years. When he didn't follow up with a threat to get me kicked out for stealing, I threw him a thumbs up and stumbled away, hardly believing my luck. I know now what an act of generosity that had been on his part, for surely he *had* seen me nick the condiments. But back then, I marked it as another bonus that came with the boothie life. You could get into the festival a day early, stay a day late, and you could barter for practically anything.

The summer music festival circuit in Alaska inspired everyone differently. Some were in it for the music and the scenery, others the late-night parties. The vendors were into a little bit of everything, as long as they made money. Only the coldest, rainiest weather sent them packing, leaving a wet hole in the protective circle of booths where the fry bread stand used to be. The sweep of marsh grasses and nearby mountains emphasized how little our absence meant to the land beyond our human enclave.

Like a circus caravan, everyone at a folk festival had a purpose: setting up booths and bandstands, taking down booths and bandstands, buying, selling, babysitting, performing, broadcasting, watching. There were cooks, and there were volunteer medics, and there were officials to oversee the whole thing. Plus our little family band.

On cold days festival-goers huddled together under the music pavilion, swaddled in wool and fleece and raingear. On warm days everyone traded layers of clothing for layers of bug dope and unfolded camp chairs in the sunshine. No place I've ever lived has felt as good as that.

Tekla and I did a little bit of everything over the years, from peddling wares to babysitting and performing. It was Camden who first showed us how to befriend the boothies. He'd learned the *way of the boothie* out of sheer, bug-eyed hunger. He popped up one time with a tray of hot fries so unexpectedly that Tekla nearly snatched him out of his shoes.

"Where'd you get those?" she'd asked. Camden shrugged, little fingers covered in ketchup. "I asked the guy with the burgers for some fries, and he said sure if I took the trash out." After that, it was game on. Boothies were forever needing pee breaks, and little errands run. When you added it up over four days, that might earn you a small treat from their booth, like a hacky sack or a coin purse or a cheeseburger.

Before we figured out the boothie game, Tekla and I had dabbled in our own little business at the Talkeetna Bluegrass Festival for a couple of years in a row, weaving friendship bracelets. The Hell's Angels were our biggest customers.

In other parts of the world, the Hell's Angels inspired a level of terror I didn't understand. To my mind, the Alaskan brothers seemed a sentimental bunch. I've since heard stories of the drug-fueled mayhem and whiskey-soaked debaucheries that ultimately killed the Talkeetna festival. As a kid, all I saw were mustachioed men in black leather who were inclined to tell me about their families and occasionally slipped me a fiver instead of a single for a fifty-cent bracelet.

I remember one biker: thickset, with a drooping gray Yosemite-Sam mustache and a wobble in his walk. He picked out bright colors for his bracelet and regularly stopped by my camp chair in sight of center stage to watch me make the ten-string monstrosity that required a lot of over and under knots. Finished, at last, I wanted to hand the bracelet over and hunt up new business, but this biker got down on one knee and hoisted me up on the other one while I tied the bracelet at his wrist.

"I had a daughter your age, once." His wrinkles took on a red and white cried-out look. His breath recalled the dumpster behind the Red Dog Saloon in Juneau: old food, ashtrays, stale beer bottles, a note of vomit. "She wasn't a redhead like you, though." He stroked my hair, which was long and ratty and more orange than red.

I didn't think about the way his hand in my hair gave my lungs a squeeze until I'd curled up in our tent for the night. He'd left me with a ten-dollar tip, my first and only, and I was very busy feeling rich the rest of the day.

I'd treated myself to fry bread and hot cocoa and taken the afternoon off to read comics in my camp chair while one fiddle-heavy bluegrass band after another wrapped up their sets. Only later did I think about what it means when you *used* to have a daughter. I wondered if that's how my father thought of me, as a daughter he used to have.

I couldn't even picture my father's face. I didn't know his phone number. I didn't know his full name. I'd gotten used to the silence where my father ought to have been. I rarely asked about him, but when I did, Mom said nice enough things. Like, oh my goodness, was he tall. And he had a big, operatic voice. Baritone. So deep you felt it in your belly when he sang. He was handsome, in love with the living world, and funny in unexpected ways. But that he led a different kind of life, one that maybe wasn't good for us. It didn't mean much to me.

Mom's booth put an end to our carefree festival times. Goodbye, long summer days spent lounging in our camp chairs with a stack of books. Goodbye, festival-wide games of chase and hide-and-seek. Hello, unpaid labor.

Now she sent Tekla and me out in sample sweaters with striped or zigzagging patterns to wind our way through shivering crowds wherever they lingered. "Boy, am I warm," Tekla would say to no one in particular. She'd rub her shaggy pink-and-purple sweater in delight while I pulled at the neck of my own blue one, scratching discreetly at the wool-induced hives.

Tekla's immunity to what people thought made her a great huckster. I envied that. For my part, the slightest tease had become a torment. At the first sign of pending humiliation, the world washed to white, and I became a petrified three-year-old. I wanted to fight, but I wanted even more to run. It reminded me too much of a man with a gun to my head, mocking me. Sometimes I still heard him at night: *You thought I wouldn't notice the way you look at me?*

I wasted a lot of wishes on a lot of stars wanting to blend in better. This was perhaps too much to ask of my jackrabbit heart, charity-bin clothes, and raggedy hair. My unusual name. My unusual family. The way we were always the new kids wherever we went.

Once I got the hang of it, I preferred hawking Mom's handmade wildflower garlands because they practically sold themselves. All winter, we'd gathered bags of drooping lichen from nearby spruce trees. We called it moose moss, though it's better known as Methuselah's Beard. We'd spent days helping Mom weave garlands together. We married fingers of bunched moss to dried wildflowers and baby's breath, and Mom deftly twisted them onto a circular rope of wire with sticky ribbon tape.

She'd worn one of her own garlands when she married C.A. the summer after we moved to Fairbanks. It had shone against her softly freckled skin like a harvest crown, a masterpiece with dried grasses whiskering out from a sunflower centerpiece woven through with pearls. She wore a cream-colored maiden's dress straight out of medieval times, and her hair fell in soft brown curls to her shoulders, complimenting her broad, gap-toothed grin. I'd tried to be happy with her, but I mostly preferred not to think about it at all.

Mom sold the half-crown garlands for ten bucks, the wraparound garlands for fifteen, kid-sized ones for five, and the proceeds went toward food (for us) and beer (for Mom). I knew they were well-loved by festival-goers, and still, the first time Mom sent us out with a pile of garlands to sell, I'd said, "What's in it for me?" I didn't want to be out there hawking wares to strangers any more than I had to, drawing all that attention to myself.

"You don't go to bed hungry," she'd said, eyeing my outstretched hand.

"One-dollar commission," I countered. Mom didn't remind me of the hard work she did every year to get us there, so I didn't concern myself with the generosity required to pay me for the little work I myself did. I didn't mind manning the booth, but chasing down sales left me with shoes full of pebbles. I didn't even know where to start.

"Look at those kids playing by the sound stage," Mom said when I balked. She sat at the edge of our booth, sipping black coffee in her camp chair, with that black Stetson hat tilted low over her eyes for shade. "I bet you get a few sales if you head over there."

Look at that. A handful of kids were, in fact, bunched up by the sound stage. They looked exactly like every pack of kids that has ever contemplated mischief since the dawn of time. The sight of them gave me sweats. "Maybe I'll go over later," I said, scratching absently at the outside edge of the butterfly painted on my cheek. One of Mom's friends was using us to drum up sales for her unofficial face-painting setup, too.

"They might be gone later," Mom countered, repressing a sigh.

"They don't really look like the garland-wearing type, Mom." Which was true. There wasn't a torn knee or mussed-up ponytail between them. They were probably camping in a twelve-person RV with built-in televisions and VCRs.

"What would I even say to them?"

Mom rolled a perfect little cigarette from the tin of tobacco she kept under her chair. "We worked so hard making those garlands pretty. I bet you don't have to say anything at all."

I'd have foregone my commission to avoid that long walk, but the flinty *snick* of Mom's lighter urged me on as I picked my way barefoot through the sawdust with a row of garlands hooked on a forearm. I angled toward the dance area in front of the stage so that on my way back, I'd pass the kids in a casual way that wouldn't require eye contact.

"Hey, did you see that?" one of the older girls said as I sauntered by. "Look at those flower things."

"Whoa," one of the smaller girls said. "They're crowns!"

"Um. Excuse me?" the older girl said, running up behind me. "Are those for sale?" She had narrow brown eyes with a touch of gold to them, and her dark hair hung in a bob that curled under perfectly. I nodded, self-consciously dragging a hand through my own hair, which I'd cut myself.

"How much?"

I pointed to the price tags.

"Can I see the purple one?"

I placed it on her forehead.

"My dad gave me ten dollars, and I don't want to waste it. How does it look?" she asked.

The girl's clothes were stylish and new. She had a neon pink fanny pack, a posse of friends, and a dad. Not just a dad, but a dad who gave her money when he took her to festivals. I would have eaten a live bat to trade places with her for a year.

"It's perfect," I said, pocketing her five-dollar bill. And another from the smaller girl, who said, "Hey, where'd you get your face painted?" Then: "What's your name? Do you live here? We're from Anchorage. I can't believe you made these garlands. They're so cool. Do you sell these all over? Hey, you want to play?"

It dawned on me that at a festival, it didn't really matter where you came from or what brought you there. The person standing next to you in line for coffee or running the sound booth could as easily be a doctor or a legislator or a librarian or a famous bluegrass picker. But you wouldn't know it from the smell of campfire in their hair or the crust of sleep in the corner of their eyes. Peddling those garlands, as hard as it had been at first, gave me my first taste of that festival anonymity.

Rich kid. Poor kid. Here we were, just *kids*. Maybe they'd never stolen condiments or had to barter with a stranger for lunch. But here they were, in my favorite place in the world, enjoying something I'd made with my own hands. As much as I ached for the kind of normalcy those girls seemed to have, I could see they had a little wonder at this wandering life of mine, too.

After that, I sauntered through festivals with our garlands on a stick slung over my shoulder hobo-style, long ribbons trailing behind me like poached rainbows. I didn't have a lot of money, but I knew all the best hiding places. I knew how to sweet-talk the boothies, and I sometimes got up on stage to sing. Back home, it took more than a few dried flowers and a butterfly painted on your cheek to fit in.

Boy Wonder & the Waterfields

~~~

Crrrrroooo-kuk, the raven outside our tent said. I sighed, blinking up at the fog of my family's breath beading on the tent wall. I snuggled deeper into the nest of sweaters and blankets we shared, but I knew I would not sleep again. That bag of feathers had been cawing for an hour already, tempting me with his curious, throaty call—a high-pitched birdish purr followed by a guttural stop, like a pebble dropped into still water. *Crrrrroooo-kuk*. I don't speak raven, of course, but my throat still tightened in response.

I liked to imagine I knew that bird from last year, but Southeast Alaska has more ravens than cars. I doubted our history.

I pounded the wool sweater I'd been using as a pillow and stuffed it back under my neck, fighting off restlessness. I wished I could lie there comfortably all day like Tekla. We alternated between calling her Princess Dynamite for her explosive temper and Sleeping Beauty for her daylong sleeping jags. Camden rarely slept past six at home. But something about the lazy summer sun filtering through the green nylon of our tent paralyzed him. He could sleep as late as eight or nine when we camped.

Mom slept on her back alongside the wall opposite me, one arm thrown up so that her wrist lay across her forehead like a portrait of Victorian frailty. I watched the muscles in her neck move in anticipation of wakefulness and the small throat-clearing cough she does.

I imagined climbing over Camden and Tekla to nestle my head in the crook of my mother's arm like a five-year-old. I wanted to press my face to her sandalwood-scented hair, kiss her awake, tell her I loved her. But I let her sleep because, at ten, I was well-versed in the landscape of her night: boozy laughter rising from the flames of one campfire after another, the high whine of fiddle and the low thump of cello overlaid by guitars and mandolins and spontaneous harmonies, clouds of pot smoke drifting toward an invisible moon in the perpetual twilight of an Alaskan summer, the low zerbert of the rainfly's zipper and her silhouette against the bug net when she woke me to turn off the flashlights we'd read ourselves to sleep by.

Through the night, my siblings had pushed, pulled, and generally spread out, leaving me with only the tattered edges of our community quilt. Now my spine pressed so deep into the tent wall that it bulged around me. Cool grasses tickled my backside through the tent wall where my T-shirt had wandered north of my hipbone. I could as easily call this tent home as anywhere else and be happier about it. Except during the cold months, maybe.

I tucked night-chilled ears under the blanket and listened to my brother's boy snores, the wind in the trees, a faraway cough in another tent. I tried to guess how many times I'd woken at the edge of a festival in this family tent. Fifty? Five hundred? But memory is slippery for a festival rat like me. I'd been spinning the fixed wheel of my mother's musical adventures my entire life. The backdrop changed often, but the tempo, the songs, and sometimes even the people were nearly always the same wherever we went.

It left me with a loose grip on time and made year markers unreliable. Home might be Juneau, Ketchikan, Sitka, Petersburg, or Fairbanks during the school year. Summers could be any combination thereof, depending which festivals or family members had the greatest pull.

Who can even remember which festival had started it all? Or count the number of summer days we slept in our own beds after that. How many black-eyed ravens had jerked me awake too early, leaving me exhausted from a long night of music and campfire, thrilled that another would follow?

I don't remember, and maybe it doesn't matter. Soon hundreds of festival-goers outside our tent were going to blink their sleepy collective eyes, unfurl shivering bodies from their own multicolored tents, and sleepwalk towards the coffee stand or the outhouses, depending. The raven's call would become background noise after the first early morning mic check from the main stage, always performed by a heavy smoker with a hangover in his throat. You'd hear, "Mic check, one-two," followed by a gagging cough and the thump of a palm on the mic to mute the spitting sound.

This is what I imagined heaven felt like; Mom, Tekla, Camden, and me in our sun-dappled tent, with another day of music warming up outside. No stepdads or visitation schedules, just us, right where we were meant to be.

Some of the kids we knew traveled all year, from festival to festival. A few of them were already touring musicians. I liked to think we could do that. We could put Camden to work as the youngest stage manager in the world. We'd suit him up in a bow tie, vest, and porkpie hat, then send him out into the crowd to summon audiences with that flaming red hair and those slate blue eyes, and he'd stay with us always. We'd call ourselves *Boy Wonder & the Waterfields*. We'd never have to worry about going home, wherever that was.

I tried not to think about home during festival season because what did it matter? Home was just a space-filler between adventures. Except every new day meant we were one day closer to leaving the friends we'd made. Kids like us with music in their bones and wildly carefree parents who didn't own televisions and insisted that we were all part of something bigger than ourselves.

I preferred pivoting around my mother's distant moon out on the road anyway. Back in our real lives, we had school and work and some variation of boyfriends and stepdads to contend with. But out here, when we had her to ourselves, it felt as if someone had hung lights from the sky just for us kids. And they spelled out: *This Is Where You Belong*.

Crrrrroooo-kuk, the raven croaked outside our tent. I wanted to unzip the front flap whisper-soft, slip into my boots, and find that bird. There were questions he could answer better than a Magic 8-Ball. It's a game I've played all my life. *Crrrrroooo-KuK*, with a rising "KuK" means yes; *Crrrrroooo-kuk*, with a declining "kuk" means no. *Will it ever be just us again?* I could ask him. *Forever?*

The Juneau Folk Festival is nothing like the other, woodsier festivals. Rather than shaking sparklers and weaving madly through a crowd of musicians around a late-night bonfire, we girls played hide-and-seek behind the black-curtained walls of the Centennial Building and tried to avoid catching Mom's eye after bedtime in case she remembered we had school in the morning. Outside, a murder of black-cloaked ravens cried hoarsely from nearby trees while all the kids formed a posse and played Red Rover, racing through slush-thickened grass in the courtyard. Eventually, a handful of us would sprawl across the boxy brown couches in the atrium and fall asleep while music drifted into the night.

The Juneau Folk Festival is a week of non-stop performances. Musicians huddle over banjos and mandolins, fiddles, guitars, and upright basses in the lobby of the Centennial Building. There are duos and family bands and a few young musical prodigies like my friend Leif Saya, a year younger than me, who knows his way around a fiddle better than a squirrel knows its tree.

World-famous musicians throng to Juneau during Folk Fest. This is why my nerves had me shaking when Tekla and I, ages nine and ten, gave our first-ever performance under our own names. We were The Little Rascals, with Mom's friends Danny Manuskin and Andy Ferguson accompanying us on guitar. We'd sung along with Mom on stage many times by then and had solos in-school performances, but we'd always been backup singers. We'd never had a set of our own before.

We sang "God Bless the Child," "Dream a Little Dream," "Sandwiches Are Beautiful," and "Be on the Lookout for a New Generation."

I'd never been nervous on stage with Mom. It's hard to have stage fright with your security blanket right there with you. I'd never really had a chance to sweat under the heat of the stage lights or appreciate the way you can only make out faces from the first five rows of an audience so big most of it is just a shadow. After the introduction, I looked out at all those strangers staring back at me, and I was so busy thinking about what to do next I missed my cue for "Dream a Little Dream." I wanted to jump in late, but I'd waited too long, and surely the audience had already figured me for a failure.

Sweat inched maddeningly down the back of my neck as people fidgeted in the front rows. Finally, I turned to Danny for help. He played through the opening again, nodded, and I jumped in. Then Tekla joined, and we alternated. We shook with nerves until the routine normalcy of singing unified us into harmony, and we found that place where our two voices sound like one. After that, we sang like we knew what we were doing.

Later, a girl my age with dark, shoulder-length hair and a pointy nose grabbed my arm as I passed her in the atrium. "You two were amazing," she said, smiling down at me. Every mistake I'd made up there replayed on a perpetual feedback loop in my brain, but realness crinkled at the corner of the girl's eyes and brought out a dimple in her left cheek. "I'm Alexis," she said, holding out her hand. Somehow I knew her as the most genuine person I'd ever met, and not only because she was my first same-age fan.

I felt sick over my mistakes, but Alexis shook her head. "It's not about how well you did," she said, all serious-eyed and wise beyond her years. "It's about doing it in the first place."

Years later, I would understand: audiences don't especially love nine and ten-year-old musicians for their performances, but for their guts. I didn't know, yet, that I could love myself for my guts, too.

It seems impossible that we hadn't heard of the Haines festival before we moved to Fairbanks. We enjoyed it so much that Mom volunteered to help organize it after our first trip. Unfortunately, this didn't cover admission for us kids, so most years, she had us roll in under the festival gate from the parking lot to get in free. It became our unofficial home base.

That's why it hit me out of the blue when Mom said we wouldn't be going to Haines the summer I turned thirteen. "It's too expensive," she said. "Ferry tickets, admission, food. We just can't do it." I didn't know she was worried about saving for an undecided future.

I moped around for a week. All winter, Mom had been absorbed in teaching private art and music classes, along with her other part-time jobs. She didn't have time to laugh with us, to play, not even to sing, except music nights at Dan Manuskin's or the Sayas' house. They were like mini-festivals anyway, and the best part about life in Juneau.

We would leave Juneau and C.A. the next spring. It would be our last festival season together for fifteen years. But I couldn't predict any of that. I only knew that things were different in Haines. There wasn't the complication of Mom's family as in Ketchikan or Thom in Sitka. And it was closer than Fairbanks, Palmer, Talkeetna, and Anchorage, all so much more expensive to travel to from the Southeast.

Mom came alive in Haines. Stress evaporated from the lines of her face the moment we unpacked the tent. She came back to us there more than anywhere else. She taught us guitar chords around the campfire, introduced us proudly to the musicians she met and dragged us onto the sawdust-covered dance floor every night.

Nothing felt more natural than when she invited Tekla and me up on the stage during performances to sing our hearts out beside her.

After Haines, there was a window of time before we lost her to the adult world. Our jokes were still funny, our pranks amusing, our enthusiasm shared.

"We have to go to Haines," I said. "We have to." She insisted we'd find something else to do. I wanted to say, *We need this, don't you understand? All of us.*

I could call a hundred places home and never sleep under the same roof for more than half a year. I could watch my mother work three or four part-time jobs while taking night classes, even help out with the cooking and cleaning and make sure the siblings got their homework and chores done. But I couldn't live forever with my mother always on the other side of the moon and only a tin-can telephone between us. Haines was our way back to each other.

Later that day, I'd walked the rocky beach in front of our house on North Douglas Island, across the channel from Juneau. I stalked the tide pools, admiring the starfish, anemones, and tiny crabs brave enough to wait out low tide in a murky mud puddle when all around were large, eager birds desperate for a tasty snack. Two ravens called back and forth from their perches in the tree line.

"Is it even worth hoping?" I asked them on my way home. One bird opened its beak and worked its tongue in a kind of laughing pant while the other chewed the underside of a wing.

Silence.

"Crrrrroooo-KuK," I called finally, out of frustration . . . *yes.*

The bird nearest me took flight, disgusted. The other one did an about-face hop and ruffled its feathers. *Crrrrroooo-KuK*, it said.

It's not hard to trick the tricksters.

Eventually, the festival director called and said, "If you come back to help, you and the kids can get in free. They don't even have to roll under the fence. They can come right on in through the gate."

Of course, my birds weren't magic. Everyone just needed my mother that much.

We only made it to the Palmer State Fair once that I remember, the summer I turned nine. It was a five-hour drive from Fairbanks and one hour out of Anchorage, where I was born. On that visit, we met a great, hulking, mountain of a man leaning against the rails at the pig races. I was too enthralled by the pigs dashing around the track in their tiny tutus to pay much attention to the new guy, except to notice the way his eyes shone painfully blue in the late summer sun and watered constantly. He wore a red beard so busy my first thought was maybe I should offer him a comb.

Looking back, it seems obvious. Something about the man's wide button nose and the wispy curls springing from his head reminded me of a friend from a dream. I kick myself even now for missing it. He introduced himself as David, kissing and hugging us like we were old friends, though surely I'd never laid eyes on him in my life. Yellow flecks stood out in his blue eyes. He smelled of garlic and onions and pot from the tiny burnt roaches in his pockets that he occasionally toked on when the crowd thinned. Sweat rolled freely from his forehead in the summer sun.

Mom's Anchorage friends were like that when they saw us for the first time. They'd start with a hug, push us back for a better look, then pull us in for another hug. They said things like, *Last time I saw you, you were a baby,* and, *Do you remember me? Your Mom and I played in the symphony together back in Petersburg.* I didn't mind. Mostly I tried to figure out how to use it to my advantage, depending on their excitement level. Were they pleased enough to buy me one of those giant cookies with M&M's? Or were they extra pumped and maybe willing to go as far as a corndog and a cookie, maybe even a hot chocolate?

Normally I'd think nothing of the man except *wow, was he strange.* But an afternoon of fair rides and greasy food and pig races—all of which David cheerfully paid for with a fat wad of bills stored in the cargo pocket of his army pants—left me concerned enough to ask as we drove away, "Who was that guy?"

I looked to Tekla to see if she knew. No help there. She'd already pressed her balled-up sweater to the window and fallen asleep with her head cocked at an angle that promised a neckache later.

Mom stopped for a red light and looked over her shoulder at me, dark brows drawn together over the crease in her forehead that she gets when she's thinking.

"David?" she said.

I shrugged.

"You don't know who David is?" she said, the crease sharpening into a question mark.

I shrugged again, recalling his red-gold curls and his wide nose.

"That was your father," she said, adjusting the rearview mirror so she could see me. The light turned green, and the car behind us honked.

I thought about this a beat and decided she was kidding. How do you spend an entire day with someone—nearly puking several times on all the candy and rides—and never guess he's your own flesh and blood? Whenever I thought of my father (basically never), he came to me as a vague legend, a storybook character called Dude from somewhere out there in the Wild World Beyond the Possibility of Knowing. I knew nothing about him except that he sold pot for a living, which was why I hadn't seen him since before my second birthday. But why would he show up now?

Whatever it meant, he was too late to protect me. Too late to be my dad. I hadn't figured out what to do with C.A. yet, and I still wasn't over Thom.

"David invited us for a barbecue in Anchorage tomorrow," Mom said casually as if nothing in the world made more sense than popping over to my estranged father's house for a warm family gathering.

The corndog and sweets he'd bought me wrestled around in my guts. I felt giddy with glut and motion sick with something angry at the same time. He'd tricked me into having a good time with him. Bought me off with junk food and rides. I hadn't even had the sense to be suspicious.

Now I'd have to admit he existed. I could no longer think of myself as a fatherless child. It felt like trying to fit a Lego into a jigsaw puzzle. My father: a real, live man. What did it mean? Did we have to let him into our family club now, the *peapod?* Why hadn't anyone warned me?

If I'd been riding in the front seat, I might have checked my reflection in the side mirror for validation. Did the yellow flecks in my eyes match his? But my mental picture of him overlapped with a biker I'd met in Talkeetna years before: the one with the Yosemite-Sam mustache. I wondered if my father had ever crouched next to a roadside lemonade stand, telling some other child my age, "I had two little girls once. Redheads."

A lone raven preened on a telephone wire outside my window as we turned off the Glenn Highway. I'd have liked to ask that bird, *Does this change everything?* But he blurred and faded, and the chance had passed almost before I knew it was there. Of course, his answer would have been *Crrrrroooo-kuk.* No. Would you even want it to?

I decided I didn't want one more thing between my mother and me, even if it was the father I'd been wondering about for so long.

"I guess we could go to the barbecue," I tried to match her off-hand tone but landed somewhere closer to tears.

Mom reached back and patted my leg.

Let's Make Some Noise

~~~

"Why don't you step out into the hallway until you can be less disruptive," my fifth-grade teacher said. "You've got a lot going on right now."

I think she was aiming for polite, but what I heard was *Big Trouble* and *You disgust me*. I clasped *Anne of Green Gables* to my chest and hung my head. How could she banish me like one of the back-row boys with their Garbage Pail Kids trading cards and their slapsticky, roughhousing ways?

No one loved quiet time more than me. I'd read every book on the class shelves in about a month, and easily half the books in the Harborview Elementary library since we'd moved back to Juneau after Christmas. Reading period gave me a taste of what gifted students regularly felt like.

I had the best spot in the room, nestled on a couch in the back of the class where I read with my instant best friend, Lily. Her parents were artists, too. She had an underbite that made taffy of her L's and R's, and I loved to hear her speak. Plus, her house was a nice break from the apartment we shared with one of C.A.'s friends.

Lily rolled her eyes when Ms. Jackson booted me to the hall like, *What are you supposed to do about hiccups, anyway? The nerve!* I shrugged, trying to muffle the noise. I let my shoulder-length hair fall across my face as I stumped across the room.

The door slammed behind me, and I marched like a good little soldier to the drinking fountain, hiccupping all the while. Big, deep gasps with a squeal at the end that actually sounded like the word "hiccup." They moved violently from my belly all the way up. Any effort to swallow them made me nauseous, so I didn't bother. I'd hiccupped every day of my life that I could recall. They varied from a single, mousy peep to long bouts, frequently lasting more than an hour. Sometimes I hiccupped from breakfast to lunch.

My hiccupping might have gone unnoticed if not for the other noises: throat clearing, sniffing, coughing. At least once a minute, the urge to wiggle my nose and sniff overwhelmed me. Not a quiet or polite sniff, either. I snorted like a wild pig on the hunt. Then the perpetual tickle at the back of my throat had me alternately coughing and ticking away with the back of my tongue, trying to scratch my tonsils. I'd met a kid once who couldn't stop jerking and jiggling his legs and had to keep moving constantly. That's how my face felt.

I slumped to the carpeted floor outside Ms. Jackson's classroom to read, but even I found it hard to do with the constant hiccupping. I could forget about the awkward sniffs and snorts, but never the hiccups. I only noticed the other noises at odd times, like during gym class or in a silent auditorium. Or when someone mentioned them, like when I'd visited Thom the summer before, and he'd nearly lost his mind.

"Sniffing and snorting is for sick people," he'd said. "If you're not sick, then this is something you can stop doing."

But what did he know? Trying to restrain the noises gave me brain-itch. The longer I resisted, the fiercer it became until it doubled, tripled, quadrupled up, burning hot as red pepper flakes down the wrong tube. I had no power over them. I might as easily swallow a tiny bomb and try to keep the explosion in. Plus, I always had to let the noises really stretch their legs after holding them in, even for a little while.

It had been easy to ignore my little noises before because everyone sniffs and coughs in grade school. But now, it seemed my fellow fifth-graders had grown out of the snotty-upper-lip phase while I had not. It left me vulnerable to quiet classrooms and auditoriums alike.

Eventually, Ms. Jackson invited me back into class, sighing. "I know you don't mean to be rude," she said. "But you're going to need to work on all this . . . " she wrinkled her nose and waved a hand around as if hoping to snatch the right word from the air between us, "stuff."

I nodded like I'd really got the message this time. Except I was actually thinking about how good it would feel to sniff so hard all the everything that had been clogging my nose since as far back as I could remember would get sucked down in one final, massive snort. I never wanted to hear about it again all the rest of my days.

I dragged myself from the hall floor slowly, gathering my book. I wiggled my nose and snorted. Coughed. Cleared my throat. Once. Twice. Three times. I hoped it would be enough to get me to lunch.

My visit with Thom the summer before had happened out of pure stubbornness on my part. I'd discovered collect calls when we moved to Fairbanks with C.A., whose presence had set me to missing Thom out loud in a way I hadn't before. I called him at least once a month, saying, *Please can I come visit?* I pestered Mom relentlessly.

"You know, you really should let me go see Thom more often," I said after every call. To which Mom responded with a sideways look, saying, "How do you think that makes C.A. feel?"

I could only shrug. Two years in, and C.A. remained a mystery to me. Anyone with eyes could see he loved my mother, the way he said, "Honey, I'm home!" when he walked in the door at night and nuzzled her neck at the kitchen sink. By contrast, I only heard resignation in his voice when he said my name, usually followed by a sigh. It hadn't occurred to me yet that maybe Mom was right, and I could improve things by keeping my sassy mouth shut more often.

"C.A. is fine," I'd say. "But Thom came first. And I miss Camden."

Thom and his new wife, Ruby, lived in the basement apartment of a giant house a good stretch out of town where my little brother had a room of his own. I'd never had a room of my own, and this seemed like the height of luxury. Camden's room had two looks: disaster or ferociously clean. This was evidence that he butted heads with his stepmother more than either of them liked. Cleanliness meant a lot to Ruby, a young Filipina who'd immigrated to America in her teens and took great pride in keeping a clean house, no matter how small or how many people lived there.

Tekla never visited Thom after the divorce. Maybe she had been too young to remember him the way I did.

I hated leaving her behind. Whenever I left Tekla to visit Thom, I always missed her more than I'd miss my own right foot if it suddenly disappeared. Until it came time to leave Thom's, then I couldn't stand the thought of leaving Camden. It's exhausting to always have someone important somewhere else to worry about.

I slept on the couch, which bothered me not at all. I had the best seat in the house for milkshakes and new *Star Trek: Next Generation* episodes, though milkshakes made me extra phlegmy and snuffly for a while. Ruby frequently paced the living room, shouting rapid-fire Tagalog into the phone, which always pinned me to the couch. I watched her more avidly than when *Knight Rider* reruns came on. I wanted to snatch her wild birdsong straight out of the air and put it in my pocket so that later I could dissect each note and learn its meaning.

Also, Ruby liked to play the entire self-titled *Wilson Phillips* album from front to back on the kitchen tape deck first thing in the morning. I thought they sounded like Tekla and I would when we grew up.

Camden and I spent our days holed up in his room constructing elaborate Lego cities and smashing them to bits with epic G.I. Joe,

He-Man, and She-Ra figurine battles. We'd barely have the last road laid down before Camden started shouting and smashing. "The city is under attack! Raaaaaaah!"

Rain fell with a constancy you could set your clock to. If you *wanted* to be outside, you could guarantee a squall. If you had dishes to do or a bed to make, the sun would invariably peep out. We made the best of dry spells, chasing each other through puddles and over mossy rocks when the clouds parted and Sitka's slanted summer sun filtered through the spruce trees. Sometimes we played ninjas, stalking each other around the property, stepping through the piney underbrush as quiet as falling leaves. I liked to imagine I had a knack for it, but Camden always found me in under a minute.

"You'd make a terrible ninja," he said, catching me for the fifteenth time. "Ninjas have total control over their bodies. They never *sniff.*"

"What do *you* know?" I said. "Have you met every ninja in the world?"

After that, I practiced stalking on my own time.

Whenever it became impossible to wring one more drop of joy out of yet another wet day, I followed Thom around while he worked. Mostly I stayed out of the way unless he asked me to assist. I handed him tools while he fiddled with a water heater or grunted over an engine. I liked our afternoons together, running into town to pick up parts, maybe grabbing a sandwich if he had a few minutes to spare.

One day the rain cleared unexpectedly. Thom had a pile of paperwork to finish, and Camden was at a friend's house. The fact that Camden had friends of his own and actually wanted to spend time with them during my visit set me to staring moodily out the window at the rare splash of sunshine we could have been playing in. Thom pushed his papers away, yawning. "Lemme show you some moves, kid."

I followed him out to the graveled driveway, where he stood in front of me to demonstrate a move. He tilted his tail bone under squared hips. Then, with his knees slightly bent, he began sweeping his arms forward with flat fists. I followed each graceful move. He slowly raised one foot and shifted forward, simultaneously pivoting while striking with his palm open, thumb folded in. Thom had studied a variety of martial arts styles for as long as I'd known him. I couldn't guess which one this was, but I loved it. I watched the precise way Thom set each foot and recalled, suddenly, the way he'd surprised me on my fourth birthday.

We'd had a costume party at our small apartment in Portland. I'd finished my costume first. Pirate, I think. Tekla had wanted to be a princess but settled for bunny when Mom promised to give her a pink lipstick heart on the tip of her nose. Mom barely fit in the tiny bathroom with Tekla propped on the sink and Camden kicking and punching inside her belly. I'd wandered into the kitchen to give Mom room to work. At the center of our little round table shone a tiny lamp, casting just enough light to save you from a broken toe but not enough to read by. Big lights were never left on in our house.

I'd pulled myself up in a chair to make shadow puppets on the wall when a slight, whispery sound behind the refrigerator set my heart thumping. I turned to peer into the darkness at the far end of the room. I saw a soft black boot with toes split in two like goat hooves and laces spiraling up a black leg that disappeared to shadow. Air rushed into my lungs with a whistle, and I held onto it, afraid I'd given myself away. Ten heartbeats. Twenty heartbeats. Then a masked face floated out of the darkness to scan the room before ducking out of sight. I recognized the black garb of the ninja from movie nights with Thom.

Ninjas, I knew, moved silent as thought. They were always sprinting across rooftops and through trees to plant a dagger in someone's heart. This one hadn't come for me, had he? On my birthday? Why?

Again, the masked face swiveled out of the dark. This time I knew he'd spotted me. He raised a single black-gloved finger to his lips. It was the longest shush of my life.

I stared at him. He nodded. We were in this together.

I thought about that for a beat.

Maybe he was a friendly ninja.

Or maybe he was Ray.

At that thought, I screamed from my belly with the kind of raw power only terror can produce.

The ninja dropped to one knee and raised his hand. Probably reaching for a throwing star. I screamed harder. He spoke then, but I couldn't hear. His words spun silver and black before my eyes even as he reached to the mask and frantically loosened it.

Footsteps pounded through the living room. The overhead lights flickered to life, revealing Mom, frozen in the doorway, taking it all in. Tekla trailed behind her in a white sleeper with a pair of paper bunny ears glued to a headband. Pink lipstick ran a shaky line from nose to ear.

A full second passed before Mom had the wits to snatch me from the chair and whirl on the ninja, who I'd finally realized was only Thom. Now I could hear him saying over and over, "Honey, it's me. Keema, it's Dad." His voice wavered between worry and laughter. "You're okay."

"Thom . . ." Mom had said, and she might have fried air with that one word.

I smiled at the memory, dragging a foot over the pebbled driveway as I copied Thom. He turned to check on my pattern and nodded, the stubble on his chin shining faintly red in the sun despite his full head of raven-black hair. "Pretty good," he said.

I knew I'd never be a famous martial artist. But I hoped he could still love me as much as his own flesh and blood.

Near the end of my visit, I laid in my sleeping bag on the couch reading while Thom and Ruby chatted in the kitchen nearby. The dishwasher purred gently, and I sucked and sawed at the back of my throat unconsciously as I turned the page.

"Do you hear that?" Thom said. I looked up in time to catch the end of a nod in my direction from Ruby.

Thom's eyes glittered as he moved toward me. His lips formed a flat line. Relaxed, but with something firm behind them, as when he'd set his teeth into finding and repairing a leak. Only as he knelt before the couch did I realize that *I* was the leak.

"Are you sick?" he asked, gently touching my arm. When I shook my head, his fingers dug in just enough to make me squirm.

"Is your nose running?"

I shrugged.

"Do you need to see a doctor for that cough?"

Shrug.

Thom's nostrils flared. I fixated on a flake of skin beside his nose to avoid his gaze because his eyes were now set on scary mode. "You. Need. To. Stop. Sniffing." He shook my arm, sending a bolt of worry through me. "Do you understand me?"

I wanted to say I'd give anything for it to stop. But I didn't know how to fix it. I didn't know why one sniff immediately required another. I didn't know why I had constant sinus, ear, and lung infections that made everything worse. I *did* know it was hard to love a girl like me. I wouldn't blame him if he decided he couldn't stand me anymore. The cough locked in my throat kept me silent for fear I'd let it go.

Thom stalked to the kitchen, back and shoulders stiff with frustration. I tried not to. I really did. But I couldn't help it. I buried my head in my sleeping bag and let out the tiniest little cough, as soft and quiet as a little mouse.

Maybe a doctor could have helped. I'll never know.

"It's basically organized crime," Mom said once (about doctors in general, and hospitals in particular). Who could afford to see a doctor for every little scratch? She preferred herbal remedies and the advice of naturopaths. She dribbled warm oil into my ears, saying, "All man-made medicine is derived from something in nature. This is as good as antibiotics and way cheaper."

The chronic ear and sinus infections were probably always going to leave me with hearing loss anyway. "Your father had terrible ear infections too," she said. I wondered if he knew we shared this family trait. "You'll grow out of them," she promised, "just like he did."

Not that the naturopaths knew what to do with all the noises. "You'll grow out of those, too," Mom said. "Strange runs in the family."

I had to keep in mind that Grandma's not-too-distant older cousins Lizzie and Emma Borden (of the famous jump rope rhyme) were pretty strange. Mom's own brothers, Neal and Toby, had a touch of the oddness, too. Neal was a ward of the state, in fact. Last anyone heard, he was a permanent resident at the Alaska Psychiatric Institute with severe psychological disorders. That was before my birth.

This did prove mildly reassuring. I may never be normal compared to my peers, but I had a leg up on a fair portion of my family.

I was seventeen when I finally got to know my uncle Toby. We both worked at Grandma Gorgeous Darling's store in Ketchikan. Like all of my mother's brothers, he was a swarthy, thickset man with dark, puffy eyes and hands so big and thick they'd break a meat grinder. Toby hummed while he took inventory, stacked boxes of T-shirts, and priced collectibles. He kept hard candies in his pocket that he snuck to me whenever I poked my nose into the stockroom, and he doted on Grandma's miniature Yorkie. You'd find them in the break room during lunch, Jolie curled into the crook of one arm, his free hand stroking her long, fine hair as he hummed old folk tunes: "Home on the Range," "Clementine," "Oh Susannah." You couldn't wish for a sweeter uncle. Still, it was hard to keep a conversation going with him because he didn't say much in general out of shyness. And when you did get him talking, he would carry on simultaneous conversations with you and other people you couldn't see.

Every so often, his neck jerked sideways, and his shoulders struck up a little jig, completely separate from the rest of his body. Boy, when he got going with his little throat-clearing routine, I had to spend five minutes in the bathroom letting loose my own sound effects just to ease up some of the pressure in my head. By then, I'd learned to soften the snorts to little sniffs, the sniffs to quick, long inhalations, the coughing to a gentle *ahem*, and I only ever tickled the back of my throat when I was alone. I wasn't cured. I'd simply learned to downplay the physical manifestations while still satisfying the urges. Nevertheless, friends found me at the grocery store, saying, "I heard your cough three aisles over, so I came to say hi."

Given my mother's aversion to actual medical doctors, it's no surprise I never heard of a nervous tic until well into my twenties. I was in my thirties before someone asked, *Had I ever noticed that my tics mimicked the sound of crying?* What on earth might have caused that kind of hurt, he wondered. The truth of it fell on me like a cure.

Inside Passage

~~~

We waited for the *all-clear* to board on a black night. The moon stitched a diamond pattern on the Gastineau Channel and glinted off the white rails of the *Matanuska* ferry so that it shone like a carnival ride. I wanted to be out there in the parking lot, stretching my legs between rows of idling cars like the young couple strolling past us with a yellow lab straining at its leash. Instead, I was trapped in the back seat with Tekla and Camden, anxious to get going. I was ten, and I took the job seriously, doling out snacks and blankets and distractions to keep Camden's four-second attention span from driving Mom nuts.

Our favorite car game:

"Mom, where are we going?" we asked in turns.

"Crazy! Wanna come?"

"Heck yeah!"

Nomads, she called us. And yet, even counting all the places we'd lived, all the tents we'd pitched, and the gas stations we'd seen, we were pretty sure crazy wasn't a place you could drive to.

You couldn't drive to most of Southeast Alaska, either, because it's made up of island communities that are protected from heavy Gulf waters by a thin strip of coast and connected by a series of waterways called the Inside Passage. To get from one place to another in the Southeast, it helped to own a plane or a boat, but we didn't have that luxury. Instead, we rode the Alaska Marine Highway, a series of merchant vessels that traverse the coastline from the northern tip of Washington to the Aleutian Chain.

Ranging from 200 to 400 feet in length, the bigger boats offered staterooms, multiple lounges, a bar, a movie theater, a playroom, a restaurant, even gift shops. Their names were grand and inspiring: the *Columbia*, the *Taku, Matanuska, Aurora, Tustamena, Kennicott*. I knew my way around each of them.

From inside our car, the Juneau ferry terminal could as easily be Ketchikan or Sitka's to my child's eyes; a small, gray building with huge windows, a parking lot big enough to fade to shadow beyond the street lamps, and a monstrous steel gangplank designed to rise and fall with the tide. Except the Juneau and Sitka terminals were set way out of town, on remote beaches with mountains rising up around them, while Ketchikan's terminal dumped you in the lower-right ventricle of the city's heart. The terminals looked the same and smelled the same. But in Sitka, I felt my brother and Thom's warm house waiting. Ketchikan held Grandma Gorgeous Darling and several uncles and cousins. Juneau, the promise of pizza and video games at Bullwinkle's.

I rolled my window down and laid my head against the frame, inhaling exhaust and treated wood and ocean. Anticipating. Ferry time was endless and cumulative; events strung together like Mom's Buddhist prayer beads. Individual trips merged into one journey so that the next morning I'd recall a humpback whale escorting us from the harbor, though it may have happened years before on a different trip.

Tekla and Camden were twisted up in each other like a pair of mourning doves by the time we were cleared to board. They slept with their heads crooked into one another's necks, mouths open, sleep-sweat muddling baby hairs at temple and brow.

Now that we'd begun to move, it didn't matter anymore where we were going or how long it took to get there. I already knew everything I needed to know. We'd board slowly, each row of cars racing at turtle speed to a designated berth in the belly of the boat. We'd park between yellow safety cones and grab our gear—a backpack apiece, a tent, Mom's cello, and guitar—and we'd race upstairs to the solarium deck to find a place to camp in the open air.

I planned to get there before the crowd. I'd push a handful of lounge chairs aside and set our tent at the starboard rail, just at the edge of the solarium roof where the overhead heat lamps would keep us warm even as the wind and salt spray tickled the rain fly. Then I'd sprawl out on a lounge chair and tap my heels three times and laugh because there's no place like home.

In an hour, we'd be underway; decks shuddering, lights dimmed, free to roam. No school. No classmates. No popularity contests or birthday parties, or stepdads. Just three kids and a young mother and three hundred strangers going somewhere. Eventually.

We rode the ferries so often that I could find my way around them blindfolded except the captain's deck. It was invitation-only and entirely marvelous. I never passed up an invitation to meet the captain.

I loved the quiet of the captain's deck, with its sea charts and black sonar screens, three-hundred-sixty-degree windows, and men dressed in sharp white uniforms with black and gold bars stitched to their shoulders—the captain at his steering console, confident as Noah. The wraparound views up there gave the impression that the world was composed entirely of gray-blue water, rocky islands, and our boat carrying all that remained of humanity.

On the decks below, I felt myself the master of an entire floating island. But on the captain's deck, I knew myself a tourist. The crews belonged to those ships in a way I could not. I still liked to pretend I knew my way around the rest of the ship as well as any of them.

During one visit, the captain twitched his drooping gray mustache and nodded. "Orcas," he said, reaching for his microphone to make an announcement. The decks below filled up so fast you'd think he'd ordered an evacuation. People lined the rails like seagulls outside a cannery. Sporty windbreakers and sun visors whipped in the wind while a handful of kids ran up and down the walkways in search of a view. I missed the wind and the salt spray of the open deck. Still, I knew that down there I would strain to see over and around and between short women and tall men with broad shoulders just to catch a glimpse of whales I'd seen all my life.

I watched those black-and-white-finned backs roll out of the deep blue without a ripple, spout dreamily, and dip below the surface. I wanted to press my body alongside the nearest whale, wrap an arm around that fin, and go places. Anywhere. Wherever. They were behind us in a handful of breaths, pursuing whale dreams.

A single orca launched skyward at the farthest reach of the horizon; a black-and-white comma. *I've been where you are*, I said to him.

The bigger boats usually stashed a few arcade games under a stairwell or near the vending machines. You might find *Street Fighter II*, *NAM-1975*, or *Hard Drivin'*, depending on the ship. Camden beat the hell out of those games. Passengers gathered around to watch him play volunteering quarters. I say *play* and *volunteering* because I don't like to call it panhandling, though the term might be more accurate. Nevertheless, by the time he was six, Camden was already a video game wizard and practically a millionaire in my nine-year-old estimation.

When Camden rode with us, Tekla and I spent more time in the kid's play area with its bright red plastic toddler slide, despite being far too big for it. We built forts out of giant Legos, played card games, and reminded Camden to go to the bathroom when he crossed his legs and started bouncing (or twenty minutes after he drank something, whichever came first).

We never thought of Camden's *gastroschisis* as a birth defect, but it came with one unfortunate side effect: he couldn't tell when his bladder was full until it was too late. Well, so what if he occasionally had to change his pants three times a day? At four years old, he could take a radio apart and put it back together. At five, he'd already been tinkering with car parts for years. Now, total strangers spent a small fortune in quarters just to watch him play video games.

When we tired of watching Camden beat his own high scores, we moved to the movie lounge. We spread out blankets and piled up like piglets to watch *The Little Mermaid* and *Teenage Mutant Ninja Turtles* before storming the upper viewing deck to practice our ninja moves.

Some years it seemed like Tekla and I lived out of suitcases, perpetually doing homework at a lounge table on one ferry or another. I'd learned to live in the bounce, the mid-air moments, the transition. Camden lived an entirely different life in Sitka with his dad. His world held the same classmates year after year, the same town, the same family. He had the kind of dependability I both longed for and dreaded.

A lot of kids we knew came from divided homes. It seemed almost normal by then that Camden lived with us only during summer and Christmas break. Still, when Camden was with his dad, I worried he'd forget me the way Dude had. Forget that I'd changed his diapers, held his bottle for him, taught him to read.

One winter, Tekla protested as we prepared to sail to Ketchikan for Christmas. "We spend more time getting there than *being* there!"

"But getting there is half the fun," Mom said. Which is why at the start of my fifth-grade year, I could draw you a map of the Matanuska ferry—where the bar was, the lounge, the arcade games, and the kid's playroom—but I couldn't tell you the name of a single one of my fourth-grade teachers.

We were hit by a winter storm on that crossing, the worst I'd ever seen. At first, I braved sideways rain on the upper deck, mesmerized by the gnashing swirls of reflected boat light surging up with each writhing crest. Our ship bobbed steadily over and through waves that could only have been stirred up by King Triton himself.

A person could grab a railing and yell into those careless waters forever, but I soon grew tired and wet and moseyed inside. Everyone else was hunkered down in their beds, green around the gills.

I'd stopped at the map by the mid-ship stairwell, hoping to divine our location, when the boat began to list dramatically.

The deck shuddered with a surge of the engine, and faint metallic groans issued from the cargo hold far below, raising the hairs at the back of my neck. I couldn't fix my eyes on the map for even one second because it was bolted to a wall, and I was not. I suddenly wished I could be. The overhead lights flickered momentarily, and I thrilled at the thought of a power outage right there in the middle of who-knows-where, with all that wet hell around us. But the lights buzzed back to life, and I figured it for the best. Imagine stuffing a few hundred people into lifeboats in that weather.

Hall railings heaved up at me and away as the ship seesawed through the dark night. Through the starboard window to my right, I could see only furious black water chopping madly, spraying foamy spittle onto the lowest deck. To my left, the portside window showed black sky. Then everything tilted. Now there was black water through the starboard window, black sky to port. I gripped a chair bolted to the floor beneath the map and watched as an abandoned Styrofoam cup rolled twenty feet to the starboard wall in three seconds.

I stumbled back to our sleeping nest in the forward lounge. No one camped on the solarium deck in this kind of weather.

Lights were low in the lounge. A few restless folks were awake still, white-knuckled in their seats.

Tekla slept belly-up on the floor between a row of chairs with her right arm thrown back in a tangle of strawberry blonde hair, mouth open. I pushed aside a stack of books and stretched out next to her. Her chest rose and fell, but I couldn't hear her breath over the ship's groans and creaks. I held her hand in the dark and smiled up at the ceiling.

Our captain knew what he was doing.

~

The winter after we moved back to Juneau and I finished fifth grade, Tekla fourth, we were invited to join a group of musicians called Heliotroupe, traveling on a grant from the Alaska Arts Council. Tekla and I were mostly invited along as an afterthought. It was Mom they wanted. But we still felt like stars.

We performed twice daily on the ferry in exchange for passage between shows in Juneau, Sitka, Ketchikan, and Petersburg. With us were a sitar player, a stand-up bassist, a mandolin player, several guitarists, a cello player, a fiddler, a Celtic drummer with his bodhran and pennywhistle, and an actor. We took shifts in the cafeteria during lunch and dinner: stunning the diners with everything from blues to jazz to Beethoven and Irish fiddle tunes. The actor did monologues, striding quickly between tables and looking audience members right in the eye.

Tekla and I sang *a cappella*: "Boogie Woogie Bugle Boy," "When the Red Red Robin Comes Bob Bob Bobbin' Along," and "The Rose." I sang melody while Tekla took the harmony. We didn't pass a hat around, but people still folded ones and fives into our hands, gushing. One woman, plump with cropped hair fading to pale yellow, held our hands as she gave us each a dollar.

"I used to sing," she said. "I gave it up. I don't know why." She shook our little fists, clenched tight around the money she'd offered like we were afraid she'd take it back. "Don't you girls ever give it up." The look in her eyes made me feel special and sorry.

Between shows, the solarium deck transformed into something like a mini traveling folk festival. On cool days, heat lamps burned the backs of our necks beneath the half-open solarium roof. Lounge chairs spread out in a widening circle as music jams warmed up, sparked by as few as two chords laid side by side. Strangers left cameras with their spouses and borrowed a guitar or a fiddle. Splinter groups formed when the sun shone so that walking from starboard to port was like setting a radio to scan: old-timey jazz, blues, rock, the thump of a bodhran, and wail of a fiddle.

Most memorable of all was my mother practicing alone near the aft rail: cello between her knees, staring into the frothy sea as it parted, swelled, and returned to itself. Tendrils of hair whipped her cheeks as she gazed into the faraway place the music always took her. I wondered what she read in the ocean's bright sea-foam braille.

I usually let her be in those moments. But this time, I climbed the rail beside her; high enough the Purser would threaten (again) to leave me at the next port if he saw me up there. I leaned into the mist and watched islands swim up beside us—close enough to count twigs tangled in the seaweed—before fading into the horizon.

"Keema, get down from there," Mom said, without even seeming to look my way. I dropped one foot back to the trembling deck but left the other on the second rail as though I'd forgotten it up there.

Every crop of land offered new possibility. I didn't know how to swim, but surely I could make it if I tried. One more step, a hard dive out and away, angling through the current precisely so: a new home, just like that. I'd eat seagull eggs and weave a net from seaweed and grass to catch fish. I'd build my own boat from fallen trees. And a hut. If I had just one place to call home, maybe I wouldn't mind being somewhere awhile. Maybe on my own private island, I wouldn't even miss this ferry life. The only thing I considered certain and true and steady as she goes.

I marked how long it took for the place I'd lived so short a time in my mind to become a thin pastel line between sky and sea. *I've been there*, I thought as each island became memory. *I'm somewhere else now.*

It occurred to me to wonder if I was woven as deeply into my mother's story of herself as she was woven into mine.

We pulled into Sitka for our final show before the night's sloshing rain had decided whether to stay or go with the morning. Sitka offers the only port that actually faces the Pacific Ocean, though you travel halfway around the island to reach it by boat. Through Chatham Strait, Peril Strait, and Neva Strait, until Olga Strait finally dumps you into Sitka Sound. The sound is protected by Kruzof Island from the harshest weather and is full of wildlife: anything the ocean washes in and everything the mountains slough off. It's not uncommon to see whales, sea lions, sea otters, porpoises, fish, brown bears, deer, and birds of all sizes while pulling into the terminal. Eagles always drew huge crowds on deck. I didn't mind eagles, but in Alaska, they're as plentiful as seagulls and about as exciting.

We were a ragged bunch by then. Twelve tired musicians in various combinations of wool, denim, and leather, with an assortment of bags and instruments strapped to our backs, stumbling up the gangplank without even the sun to light our way. The February air hung thick and moist and heavy with harbor smells that slapped the sleep from our eyes.

Camden met us at the terminal with Thom. I smooshed my lips into his cheek and reluctantly gave him over to Mom before turning to Thom and making a running jump into his arms. I wanted to tell him everything in my heart, all the things he'd been missing out on. But I only said, "I missed you."

He gave me a sideways grin. "I missed you too."

I didn't mention that even though he'd left with Camden four years ago, I sometimes still crawled into Tekla's bunk to hold her while she slept. If anyone ever tried to take her, they'd have to take me too. I didn't tell him that I missed Camden so much that it felt like a punishment.

Thom dropped Mom and the rest of the troupe at the Unitarian Church and took us girls home to hang out before our show at the Sitka Performing Arts Center. Our preparations included Kung-Fu movies and *Star Trek* re-runs, homemade milkshakes, and Camden trailing his favorite Legos through the living room like a puppy with a special squeaky toy. I pretended we were a family again. Just for the day.

Thom sat through as much of the show as he could after we finished our sets, but the performances stretched on and on, late into the evening. The auditorium was still packed long after the early birds flew home for bed. There were people in the crowd we'd met on the ferry. They'd probably spent the day touring St. Mary's, the first-ever Russian Orthodox cathedral built in America, or Tongass National Park.

The night carried us to an after-party somewhere because the music never ends. It left me almost too tired to cry at the sight of Camden's small face pressed to the car's rear window when Thom waved us off at the ferry terminal two days later. Camden laid one small hand flat against the glass, pleading for us to stay. As much as I envied him waking in the same place every day, going to school with the same friends year after year, walking familiar streets, it promised its own kind of loneliness, too.

We were the last to board, hustling down the gangplank as fast as our legs could carry us. I didn't have time to notice the tide or the sun stretching catlike across the Pacific or to feel what it meant to leave yet another place I loved. People I loved. I tossed my bag in a lounge chair on the solarium deck and ran to the forward bow. I climbed the railing and pretended my face was wet with ocean spray. The thing to do was to look ahead: tomorrow we'd be at Grandma's in Ketchikan, and a few days after that, Petersburg.

Seagulls rode the thermals above my head until we picked up speed and left them behind. The rail hummed, and red hair swirled madly around my face as we entered Olga Strait. I refused to look back. I knew that Sitka was already a thin pastel line on the horizon.

I kept my face to the wind.

Pinned to the Rocks

~～~

I'd been stocking groceries at the health food store in Juneau when it happened: *weakness*. Suddenly I could not lift a six-pack of root beer into the sweating refrigerator before me. My arms were useless clubs. The kind that haunt you in bad dreams where you try and try to swing at the world's fastest bad guy, but your body responds in slow motion. Legs trembling, back aching, stomach doing loop-de-loos, I set the pop down and felt for fever sweats on my forehead.

In the bathroom, I discovered a few things about womanhood that I wasn't prepared for at barely eleven years old. First, there's the horror of it. This was immediately followed by a shock of recognition and the fear of being found out. And finally, a jolt of giddiness.

Then there's the reality of it: it's messy.

I ran stiff-legged two blocks to the boarding house where my family of five shared a single rented room because it was summer and Camden was with us. I burst through the front door and smack into a group of slit-eyed musicians. Mom was the only woman among them. The interior hit me like a smell attack: worn leather couches, body odor, stale incense, and pot smoke, all of it mixed with the tang of metal strings, musty guitar cases, and the fresh zip of rosin on Mom's bow.

Mom had the fiddle to her neck. The bow arced and dipped, arced and dipped. She had the faraway eyes of a dreamy jam session, but I sidled up and tapped on her shoulder anyway. I leaned in to whisper my news in her ear and waited. She nodded. This was an acknowledgment that someone from reality was at the door, and she knew she must find her way back from the tune. It seemed a long time before she recognized me.

I stood before her, jutting my hips out like a model: ready to celebrate. Surely being able to make a baby was a beer-worthy event. Heck. I already had an occasional job! Yes, I had to work under the table because eleven-year-olds weren't technically employable. Still, I'd soon own a house and would not share it with roommates. Maybe I'd upgrade my job and start working as a trail guide or move back to Fairbanks to race sled dogs and make documentary films.

Mom squinted dreamy eyes at me, not entirely sure what I needed. Finally, she shrugged her shoulders and said, "Well, you know what to do." She absently rolled a cigarette from the tin of Drum. Maybe she thought I'd learned more than I had from overheard conversations with her friends, or the library, or an older girl at school.

I did *not* know what to do. I'd only found out this was coming in fifth-grade sex-ed class a few months before. And all they do in sex-ed is tell you it's coming: not What To Do. Then they tell you to talk to your parents about it. *Hah, hah.* Picture that conversation with C.A. right there in our shared family room, absentmindedly tugging the braided rattail that hung a foot down his neck, trying to think of something to say.

Flustered, nervous about sharing this moment with the men sprawled out on couches all around me, I whispered fearful questions in Mom's ear. *What do I do now? Will it hurt? Will I have a baby soon? Will everyone know?*

Already men looked at me differently—assessing, where before their eyes had slid off me. Women had begun looking me up and down in public, taking mental notes of my height, stringy reddish hair, widening hips. Oh, the agony of sudden boobs. I knew myself judged.

I feared the start of the new school year. Fifth grade had been embarrassment enough. I'd just gone through the pain of being the new kid yet again at Harborview Elementary halfway through the year. Now I had to add the tenderness of *the change* and the horror that my life as a tomboy would come to an end. It made the idea of middle school seem a secret new level of hell. I'd rather go straight to college. Maybe there I could count on being treated like a person rather than a child.

People my age were kids in a kid's world. What did most of my classmates know about fighting with drunks, worrying about food money, standing between siblings and stepparents? Most of my friends couldn't even cook the easy stuff: soup, pasta, oatmeal. I couldn't imagine them making their own lunches, changing diapers, bandaging wounds. One day in second grade, I woke up, and the plain fact of it had slapped the fuzzy dreams from my head: I was a grown-up in a kid's body. Always the wrong age.

I tried sometimes to talk to my mother about it. But I couldn't seem to reach her anymore. A secret switch had flipped during the move back to Juneau from Fairbanks, leaving her on autopilot and us kids hungry for the way things had been before we left Juneau. For one thing, I didn't remember her keeping company with so much cheap beer before we moved back from Fairbanks. And she'd quit making dinner for another. "C.A.'s an excellent cook," she said, overriding our objections. "I've cooked enough for a lifetime, raising those kids," meaning her brothers and sister and all the responsibilities she herself had as a girl.

My mother hovers, silent and ghostly, at the periphery of my memories from the six years we lived with C.A. We didn't talk as often about my friends at school or the books I read. We barely talked at all. I wanted to play with her the way we used to, telling her awful jokes I learned at school about boogers and making her laugh until tears leaked from her eyes and she begged me to stop.

Where before we could drag her into our imaginary games, spending time with our mother now meant endless hours of quiet absorption. She laughed the most when playing music with friends. Otherwise, I'd grown to expect her quiet eyes to be busy elsewhere. She rallied to send us off for chores and to bed. And in exasperation, to mediate fights.

We couldn't fling ourselves into bed with her at the crack of dawn and snuggle into her warm side anymore for fear of waking C.A. in a hopping, spitting fury. It hurt that the small hopes and heartaches of our childhood seemed unable to reach her.

I blamed C.A. for changing everything. "You're not my dad," I told him at every opportunity. He didn't play with me or watch *Star Trek* or encourage me to think about the world. The way I saw it, he'd married my mother and commenced bossing me around without bothering to win me over. I knew it could be different because it had been with Thom. Personally, I didn't see why we needed C.A. around at all. It never occurred to me that I could befriend C.A. myself. That maybe our lack of bond came from his not knowing how and my own childish assumption that he didn't want to be close to me. "It takes two to tango," Mom loved to remind me when C.A. and I shook fists at each other. But I never gave C.A. anything but a stubborn kid's heart.

"Why can't it just be us?" I'd finally asked when we moved into the boarding house. Mom had already bought a renovated school bus that we'd soon be living on. "Us kids and you?"

We were on our way home from the grocery store with dinner supplies. Mom stared through a red light, her black Stetson hat pointing straight ahead. She didn't frown, and she didn't smile; just stared through the traffic ahead of us. I noticed that she didn't have wrinkles yet, like some of the other moms I knew.

"Oh, Keema," she said after a while, the weight of her world in my name. "You don't know how lonely I would be."

I didn't know. I hadn't, in all eleven years of my life, known the hardship of raising kids alone. I'd never felt loneliness except in the absence of my mother and siblings. I didn't like to think it, but some part of me knew I had a classic case of Petulant Child of Divorce Syndrome. At the time, I only wanted to know why we kids weren't enough. I wanted to know what our stepdads and the boyfriends had that we didn't have. But the faraway look in Mom's eyes reminded me of the way she looked playing music: unreachable. So I didn't ask. And she didn't say.

Years later, she would tell me that after we left Fairbanks, she'd started having what she calls absent seizures. "I knew I was of the world. Alive. Part of things," she told me. "But I couldn't drag myself out of this quiet, faraway paralysis. It was like . . . I could hear you knocking, but I couldn't get to the door in time."

That faraway place became the new normal as her childhood bubbled up through her psyche. It ate away at her careful, happy, willfully free world. She could no longer escape the pain of her brother's assaults or the casual violence of her mother's old-school parenting.

That's how it went the day I started my period. Me: calling into the darkness. Her: trying to reach back. I nearly vibrated with unasked questions. Had she been scared the first time? How weird was it to have a daughter who could have a baby when she herself was barely thirty-one?

Only when she didn't immediately lay aside her fiddle at the news of my pending womanhood did the entirety of our story come clear to me: there were just going to be days when I couldn't ask for more.

I'd needed privacy and space during the summer months before I started my period. Something hard to come by the way we lived. We'd had a pretty good thing going in the house we shared with C.A.'s friend on Starr Hill. The "Dump-With-A-View" Mom called it. But our downstairs neighbors had ruined that with their nightly drumming sessions. Neighbors complained, and we'd gotten the boot in the spring along with the drummers.

After that had been a series of friends' houses. A stay with Grandma Gorgeous Darling in Ketchikan. Then our annual trek to Haines for the Southeast Alaska State Fair, where we lived in a tent, and everything was life as usual: performing on stage with Mom, hawking flowered garlands, selling Alpaca sweaters. Camden tying his pocketknife to a stick like a caveman and befriending everyone who owned a food booth.

One night, after a music party in Haines, we slept in a tepee in the host's backyard, oblivious to rain clouds gathering in the black night. We woke to a river running around us in the wee hours of the morning, our coats and bags slowly drifting through the tent's canvas flap-like prisoners bent on escape. I'd wanted to climb on the flat back of a particular black Martin guitar case and ride that rivulet someplace I could call my own.

Alas. In July, we moved into the boarding house in Juneau. Now we shared a bedroom on the third floor with giant windows and just enough floor space for two full mattresses.

Instead of privacy, I shared a bed with Tekla and Camden immediately adjacent to Mom and C.A.'s bed. C.A. was laid up with a back injury while Mom was working a handful of part-time jobs to cover the medical bills and beer while still saving up for whatever came next. We were stuck with this one room and each other. Like it or not.

The boarding house made me twitchy. Tenants came and went with the regularity of rain clouds, and that's saying something when you live in a rain forest. "Go find something to do," Mom would say when days of rainy cabin fever had us kids on the verge of doing full head rotations.

I was happier outside, anyway. Fall grasses and wild strawberries sprouted up daringly along the roadside and in the cracks between sidewalks. Salmonberries grew fat on the bush, summoning us with the promise of their tart hearts. I dubbed myself Queen and set

Tekla and Camden to gathering berries from the cruelest bushes in tribute to me. In return, I gave them my protection. And my love.

We played and fought like puppies. We roamed sunny neighborhood streets by bike and foot: screaming, singing, ringing our little bike bells. Sometimes we spent hours at the playground, finally heading home at dusk with mouths, fingers, and shirts stained purple with berry juice.

Other days I could not get out of bed.

"Let's go to the park; I'm booooooored," Tekla would whine.

"No."

"Play cards?"

"No."

"Bike ride?"

"I'm dying here. Leave me alone."

"You're such a bitch," she'd say, the little divot in her nose flaring as she crossed her arms, twin braids shaking in disgust. "What's wrong with you? You used to be fun."

I wanted to have fun. To *be* fun. To even remember what fun felt like. I didn't know about hormones yet. About what was coming.

"You can't call me a bitch. You're not even ten years old. You're just a kid."

Eventually, I learned feminine supplies were in the bathroom, and womanhood was not a beer-worthy event. A few weeks later, I made a pact with my school friend, Lily: we were going to have a grown-up adventure.

Earlier that spring, we'd found a driftwood hut while beachcombing south of town with Lily's dad, Bill. It was a sturdy little thing made of sticks and grasses packed so tightly together that it didn't even tremble when I bumped into it.

"I think it's maybe a sweat lodge," Bill said.

"Cool," Lilly said.

"Do you think we can sleep in it for a night?"

"Hmmm," Bill said. A non-answer.

It had awoken in me the same urge to nestle down in a place of my own as that snow house had back in Fairbanks. For months we begged someone to take us camping out there, but no one volunteered. Now that I could make a baby, I figured I had enough growing up behind me to adult for one night. I had a job and the cramps to prove it.

"I've got this camping thing down," I told Lily as we laid plans.

Even at eleven, I knew that survival meant food, water, clothing, and shelter. But we owned only one sleeping bag between us. I figured we could share the sleeping bag if we added trash bags over and under it for extra warmth and insulation. I knew from a life of travel to pack easy food: sandwiches, crackers, trail mix. I knew to wear a lot of layers.

Because I thought myself undefeatable, I did not bother to think about things a person might die from during a survival situation in the wilderness. Even in summer, people have been surprised by snowstorms, avalanches, falling from a high place, poisonous plants, hypothermia, gangrene, starvation, bears, drowning, freezing, giardia, and falling into a crevasse or through snowpack into a river. Stupidity covers a lot of ground too.

Two weeks before sixth grade began, Lily and I packed our sleeping bag and trash bags, some water, a can of olives, a few slices of bread, apples, crackers, and cheese. I felt pretty good about things.

"It's not technically running away if we say where we're going," Lily said.

"Right. We'll totally leave a note," I said.

"We just won't tell them we're going until we're gone," Lily agreed.

At the last minute, our friend Sidra joined us with her pet rats; a giant black-and-white spotted mama rat the size of a woman's shoe and two babies. Tekla wanted to join us, but I said no. I couldn't be taking care of her too.

~

We trooped fearlessly out of town, utterly confident in our ability to rough it this one night. We held hands and skipped in the middle of the road and then, laughing, hid among roadside pine trees and devil's clubs whenever cars passed.

We'd walked for an hour when Lily said, "Who's hungry?"

We stopped to eat the can of olives beside a waterfall so small it would be better named a waterdrip. After another mile of rocky gray beach, we started to worry that maybe the hut had been torn down.

"Was it a mirage?" Lily wondered aloud. Had we missed it? But minutes later, we spied it up ahead.

It was as firm and round as I remembered it, with a nice sandy fire pit in the middle. Were the entire structure dropped onto a river, you might mistake it for an extra-large beaver dam. The hut sat in a rocky alcove that jutted skyward twenty feet or more, nearly a cave, but open to the sky at the top. I liked to imagine it dated back centuries.

The beach around us offered a lot of rock and shale but very little sand. Long ropes of dried seaweed snaked across the shore and piled up at the base of the cliffs around us. Crushed shells and bird bones lay scattered like buckshot all around us, but the higher debris was old and brittle. I assumed this meant the tide rarely climbed as high as our hut.

I lit a fire easily enough, though the beach wood we scavenged was wet, and the fire smoked more than it blazed. I knew how to make a wood stove roar, but exactly nothing about waterlogged driftwood. We tried to grill cheese sandwiches over a warm, flat rock but were too impatient. We settled for moist bread with warm cheese in the middle.

After that, it was dark, and we were bored. To our surprise, the beach had neither television nor radio. It hadn't occurred to us to pack a deck of cards. The stars were hidden by fat clouds, and the moon didn't bother showing itself. Camping at festivals, you always had the twitchy light of distant fires and the faraway thrum of a guitar. Out here, with the tide so low we couldn't see it in the dark, we didn't even have the luxury of gentle ocean sounds to absorb us.

We were three girls on the hunt for adventure with nothing but a dull, gray-black sky and a few rats to stare at, and the rats were edgy. It was all we could do to keep hold of them without breaking their tiny ribs. I wondered out loud how well they'd do if we let them go.

"They're pets!" Sidra said. "They've never even fed themselves."

Wouldn't instinct kick in, though? Wouldn't a tiny, wild, animal voice shout orders? *Build a nest. Forage for food. No, not that kind; this kind. Hide from big things with teeth.* I thought it would be interesting to release one of them and come back every week to visit. Would it remember us? Would it find a mate out there in the rain forest? Somehow, I didn't think rats were native to the island.

None of us admitted our disappointment. What had we expected? S'mores and Northern Lights would've been nice, at least. Maybe a little music. We wouldn't have said no to a real bonfire either.

With nothing else to do, we bedded down early to tell half-hearted ghost stories. Our hazy little fire gave off a lot of smoke, but only very little warmth. Sidra took the sleeping bag since she had to keep the rats warm, while Lily and I curled up in the trash bags and shivered. I'd tried to dig up the biggest stones so we'd have mostly sand to lie on: softer and easier to heat with our bodies. I'd also piled dried seaweed from around the hut into three little pallets. Cold rocks dug into our hips and backs anyway.

I slept fitfully, waking sometime later to a new sound among the crashing waves that gulped hungrily at the beach. The water was now half again as close as it had been when we arrived. I couldn't see the water, but I could feel it. The nearness of the ocean startled me, as it often had when I was very little. How could one little stretch of beach change so drastically every few hours?

At first, I couldn't make out what had woken me. The sound came again in a lull between waves. The faint click of rocks knocking together carried on the wind. A tiny sound amplified by the cliff walls behind us that carried on the wind.

Suddenly we were all awake and clutching each other. Whispering:

Bear.

Be quiet. It'll hear you.

You think it's a bear?

Shut up! Shhh. Oh my god.

We're going to die.

Why hadn't we thought of bears?

I realized we were trapped. Betrayed by this enticing sweat lodge and its false sense of security.

The crunch of beach rocks colliding drifted slowly toward us, and we girls huddled tight as a pent-up scream. I stared at the dark beach, forcing my eyes wide open. I wanted to see my killer before I died. We waited for the danger to show itself as the ocean slowly chewed away the shoreline before us, one contemplative bite after another. We waited so long the sun might have expired, and the earth devolved into space debris.

Finally, something showed against the black sky. Far away, a small white bouncing disc hopped around the beach like a sand flea. We trembled silently. Then the disc of light became a beam of light and resolved into a flashlight. Now our thoughts were of boogiemen and disappeared children.

Why had we not thought of murderers?

I decided bad guys were better than bears because I could confound bad guys and help my friends escape. It seemed the least I could do after dragging them out there.

We lay still, not even daring to breathe, until two figures emerged from the darkness: Lily's dad and her brother, Kahlil. I let out more air than I'd known my body was capable of holding. Bill strode across the beach as calm as if it were noon, and we'd planned to meet there all along.

"Ladies," Bill greeted us, shining the flashlight on each of us in turn. He stood silent for so long I began to wonder if he was waiting for an invitation to join us. "Did you happen to check the tide table before you left?" I looked up at him from my garbage bag, blinded by the flashlight, shaking with cold and leftover fear. We shook our heads dumbly, unsure whether to get up. Bill cast his light around the little hut, pointing out dried seaweed and debris.

Now that he mentioned it, I *had* noticed the seaweed that drooped from the driftwood walls of our hut-like moss. I simply hadn't paused to consider how it got there.

The year after our doomed adventure, the news of Chris McCandless' death made headlines in the *Juneau Empire*. His story knocked me sideways. Here was a young man found starved to death in a bus out on the Stampede Trail, north of Fairbanks. According to early reports, McCandless died because he'd been inadequately prepared for his trip. He didn't know the terrain, or how to skin a moose, or which plants were safe to eat. He didn't have a guide. Only instinct. By all accounts, he'd simply walked out into the wilds of Alaska, expecting to master it somehow. I kept thinking, *How could anyone be so naïve?*

The romance of his adventure tugged at something I couldn't pin down, even as his death haunted me. Involuntary tears sprang to my eyes whenever his name came up.

"Why does his story seem so extra sad?" I asked Lily.

"It could have been us," she said. The truth of it was a heartache I hadn't dreamed of when we'd plotted our course.

I imagined her dad calling my mother, telling her *The girls are gone.* Then the debate: *Were we safe out there for one night? Should someone go after us?*

"We thought about letting you have your misadventure," Bill had said when he found us on the beach. "But tonight is the highest tide of the year." The bright disc of his flashlight arced up the rock face behind us to illustrate his point.

I didn't see the problem right away. Surely the tide wouldn't come so far up as this? But then a little voice in my head said, *Where'd you think all that seaweed you're sleeping on came from, dummy?*

We crawled from our beds slowly. I examined the cliff wall behind us, revealed now by a moon that had crept out from behind the mountains. Above us, tufty fingers of dried seagrasses clung to crevices, hung from ledges, wagged in the wind like a warning. *You should not be here, no, no, no.* Part of me wanted it to be a message for someone else. Someone younger and more foolish. Part of me wanted to dig my heels in and surrender my shame to the seaweed. Bill could take the girls; I'd stay with the rising tide and suffer the consequences. Maybe I would survive it like I'd survived everything else: by sheer willpower.

Bill never raised his voice. He stood silent in the dark while we packed our things, though my arms felt as useless as they had a few weeks earlier at the health food store. I couldn't bear to look at Lily or Sidra.

Willpower would not have saved us. That tiny, wild, instinctive voice I counted on had never made a peep.

As I gathered my things under Bill's watchful gaze, an image came to me of three little girls waist-deep in salt surf, trying to climb the cliff face for hours and hours. Three little bodies pinned to the rocks by a crashing tide. Three little bodies swept out to sea.

Learning Curve

~⁓⁓~

At the end of fifth grade, Lily had called out of the blue and said, "Do you want to homeschool with me and my friend Jeramie next year? Our parents can take turns teaching us."

I'd turned to Mom and said, "Do I want to homeschool next year with Lily and Jeramie if our parents all take turns teaching us?"

Mom had laughed and said, "No, you do not. I have four different jobs already."

"That's a hard maybe," I'd said into the phone.

Honestly, homeschool might have lost its appeal over the summer if not for the bus. Mom drove us out North Douglas in June to look at it. Someone had spray-painted the thing seaweed green so that it rose like a defeated bog monster from a wide, graveled driveway just off the highway. Dead car batteries and rusted-out washing machines erupted from the knee-high grasses and mud surrounding it. Pine needles and tree branches littered the roof of the bus, which had been extended by two feet for extra standing space and a hunchbacked effect. Rain sheeted over the windshield to pool in broken headlight casings before dropping tearfully into giant puddles beneath the front tires, which were flat.

"Where would we park it?" I asked.

"Well, the brakes don't work," Mom said, "but the owners of the house say we can stay right here."

"Are you serious?" I kicked a flat tire. The only useful thing I could imagine about living on a bus would be the freedom of wheels, and this thing didn't even drive. I could see us ferrying into a festival with it, though, rolling up to the campground like royalty. We could leave the tent behind entirely.

But the bus could not even handle so basic a task as braking. It inspired my homeless heart not at all.

"If we move onto that thing, I'm not going back to school," I said. "I get enough grief."

"It's only for a little while," Mom said. "Just while we save up to make a down payment on a house. Besides, what are you so afraid of? Kids tease you because they like you. And they're mean because they're jealous." When pressed, she had only vague ideas about just what exactly kids might be jealous of. "Well, you're really smart," she said. "Everyone wishes they could be smart, even when they act like being an ass is cooler."

I didn't know a lot about being a pre-teen early bloomer, but I damn sure knew that one thing kids my age weren't jealous of was smarts. They might be jealous of your Reeboks, or your Lego collection, or your Super Nintendo, if you were lucky enough to own any of those things. But I never heard a person say, "Gee, I wish I had a big ol' nerd brain." And not once, in almost two years on the bus, did a single kid say to me, "Wow, it's so cool that you live on a bus."

It's not like the Green Machine was entirely unlivable once we settled in. There was a reading bench up front behind the driver's seat, which was the only seat left because, well, you'd need it for driving if the brakes were ever fixed. The windows were drywalled over and painted white. The rest had been converted entirely to living quarters.

Rows one-to-five became our living room, with a slim reading bench facing a tiny wood stove. Rows six-to-twelve held a small built-in kitchen on one side and cupboards on the other. A triple-decker bunk bed occupied the rear, rows thirteen-to-eighteen. In a rare fit of generosity, I'd have likened it to living in a deformed plywood R.V. dressed up as a school bus and painted a nauseating shade of green.

For Mom, bus life was a chance to appreciate the little things. Like the tiny wood stove that kept us toasty most of the winter. And the honey bucket that saved us from running out to pee in the snow every hour but also made the place smell like an outhouse. She might have been born too late to qualify as a real hippie, but my mother's heart still beat to the drum of the back-to-the-earth movement.

Tekla and I were a long way from developing the fine art of appreciating the little things, though. We finally had a chance to stay put for a time. And it was on a *bus*.

"You'll remember it fondly when you're older," Mom said.

When we pointed out that our living arrangements had basically ruined our social life *already*, she said, "Whatever doesn't kill you makes you stronger." I recognized this as code for, *Kid, just be glad you're not forced to work a coal mine every day.*

We didn't necessarily want to be stronger. We just wanted some of the luxuries other kids in America had. Even a lot of poor ones like us. A shower, for instance. A real toilet instead of a bucket with a seat on it. Maybe a bathroom door instead of a thin privacy curtain. My fantasies could even stretch as far as cable television.

I determined not to set foot in Marie Drake Middle School as long as we called the bus home.

Looking back, I don't recall a particular incident from fifth grade that made me anxious about middle school. I can't imagine my fellow fifth-graders were worse than any year before, children being equal opportunity monsters at every age. Except that now I was the first girl in my grade with boobs and a period. And I lived on a *bus*. You might as well paint a bullseye on my chest.

I felt myself ill-equipped for this new level of hippie living. I couldn't yet name the terror I felt when kids teased me. Sure, the first time I'd ever heard sarcasm, there'd been a gun aimed at my head. But I didn't think about that every time a classmate spat in my face or spiked a dodgeball at me while their friends laughed. *You're so stupid. Don't you know you're supposed to get out of the way?*

I owned only panic in those moments.

The rest of the time, I yearned for the invisibility of normalcy. Maybe they'd notice me less if I didn't stick out like an enormous piece of driftwood on a sandy beach. But it takes a long time to become sand, so I took a break from public school instead.

Homeschooling does about as much for your street cred as living on a bus. Still, Lily, Jeramie, and I thought we had the best thing going in town.

Jeramie, a fisherman's son with dirty-blond hair, slate-gray eyes, and dimples, wore rubber boots every single day I knew him. These he paired with a vest and a short-billed painter's cap that looked like it should sport a propeller. He had small teeth with a gap like Madonna's, which gave him a roguish grin. He lived with his dad on a houseboat out in the Gastineau Channel. To reach their house, we piled into a skiff and rode out of the protective marina barrier into the choppier water beyond.

The houseboat was just that: a house plopped down on an old barge. I don't remember it being *damp,* but I do remember it being dark. The lights, the television, the refrigerator, all of it was powered by generator. This casual use of electricity with the ocean all around us went against everything I knew about hairdryers and bathtubs. At least on a ferry, you were above the water with a thick steel hull to protect you from big waves and breaching whales. Fortunately, we rarely had school there more than once a week.

Jeramie had more Legos than Douglas Island had spruce trees. I knew enough to be impressed by his collection, but not enough to construct things like a professional Lego architect. "No, no! You build the spaceship with the grey and red pieces. Here, you obviously need it spelled out for you because you're a girl. Read the instructions," he'd say. And if I followed the instructions perfectly, he'd say, "Pretty good." Then we'd hide under his bunk bed to kiss, thrilled by our collaboration. A disproportionately high percentage of our school days on the barge went like that.

Mom's school days usually entailed nature walks and philosophical debates, so we were hardly on the bus itself. She was experimenting with a collage technique at the time, and she trained her camera on us through every outing. Afterward, she painted sheets of rice paper with watercolors, then glued colored strips of it onto a canvas and painted over them. The bulk of her paintings from that year depict three figures in raincoats walking the Douglas Island shoreline: Lily, Jeramie, and me.

Instead of the chaos of regular classrooms, our lessons involved hands-on experience. For math, we had a lunch budget. Science activities ranged from growing bean sprouts and avocados to designing and building complex dioramas to scale.

The mountainside behind Lily's house offered a small fortune in ripe salmonberries, ranging from orange to purple. We sang as we bucketed them, as much for amusement as to warn nearby bears. Lily preferred knock-knock jokes to singing. It got so that you heard her mind click into joke mode and said, "Who's there?" quick before she even warmed up. Then we hauled our stash down to the docks in small paper cups to sell to tourists while cruise ship season lasted. We ate half as many as we sold.

The cruise ships that lined the dock across the street from Lily's house from late spring through early fall were like self-contained cities. They sailed in with their lights twinkling day and night, and then hordes of people poured off the docks and into the streets like a slow-moving mudslide. Sometimes I wanted to run screaming through their midst, yelling, "Fire! Fire!" just to see how long it'd take to get their attention.

The people who stopped to ask about our berries made up for the millions who never noticed us. And you might have mistaken me for royalty the way I strolled into J&J Deli for candy with all that loose change rattling around in my pockets during berry harvest.

We spent the bulk of our school time at Lily's. She lived in an actual house and had two parents that were still together. Musical instruments hung on her walls, and it always smelled like lunch when you walked in the door, even early in the morning.

Lily was an exact replica of her mother, Clarissa. Standing side by side, you'd mistake them for sisters. Hardly more than five feet tall, they both had long black hair, deep-set brown eyes, and smooth skin.

Lily's mother was forever sewing buttons on enormous black-and-red blanket robes, the kind worn during traditional Tlingit ceremonies, as they were Ravens, of the T'akdeintaan clan. This might be why Lily specialized in play ceremonies. One time she danced in a robe her mother had made, singing. I didn't understand the song, but I felt the spirit of it.

"There!" she said, bright and crisp. "You are an honorary member of my family."

I knew it for playtime, even as part of me ached for it to be real.

Lily's father led the bulk of our class time. Bill was a musician and artist, and he owned the kindest eyes I'd ever seen. I never once saw him upset, not even the night he rescued us from our campout on the beach. He barely raised an eyebrow the time I chiseled a chunk out of my left index finger while carving wood in the basement. When I thumped up the stairs, barking like a seal in my pain, he'd prodded the flap of muscle and skin, nodding. "Stitches for you," he'd said, swiping car keys from a hook by the door.

I refused. I'd been lazy with the carving tools, and I knew it. We could barely afford to live on a *bus*. I wouldn't give my mother the burden of an emergency room visit for anything less than an actual limb that needed reattaching. Bill clenched his keys but watched calmly as I leaned on the sink, absorbed by the bright blood spiraling down the drain. He stood beside me until the bleeding slowed, then silently handed me duct tape and gauze to wrap the wound in. He offered no judgment or reproach. Only presence. I wished I could pocket a single ounce of that calm to carry it around with me forever.

On our first day of school, Bill had given us a recipe for bread. "Memorize it," he said. "You're going to eat a bunch of it." We baked huge batches of bread once a week thereafter. We cooked all of our own meals. We stirred up sauces, made our own noodles, and pitched a few truly inedible failures on the compost heap that year.

One morning we sent our math papers flying and scrambled outside to coo over a black bear cub rooting through leftover spaghetti out in that very compost heap.

"What's it eating?" Jeramie asked.

"How'd it get there?" I asked.

"Where's its mother?" Lily asked, backing slowly toward the door. We knew better than to stand between a sow and her cub.

The cub was hardly bigger than a three-month-old Labrador, too skinny and too young to be wandering on its own. We watched him for an hour, but no vengeful, tooth-bearing mama bear turned up. Bill helped us figure out how to report the cub to Animal Control, and while we waited for help, he explained the complications of human and environmental interactions. The way he laid it out, things went like this:

humans = garbage
garbage = bears
garbage bears = dead bears.

This had us all crying murder.

"We called someone out here to *kill* this starving little baby?" I didn't calm down even when Bill explained that the cub would likely go to a zoo and live a happy life. I had to know for sure. I plotted the number of steps it would take to snatch the cub and run like hell. I wanted to release it in the woods somewhere safe from idiots like me who threw my food outside to rot and attract orphaned babies who'd then be shot.

We each had our own way of dealing with it. Jeramie dwelled on the cub's chances of finding a zoo, while Lily did a blessing, inviting protection for him. I readied myself for war. A war the Animal Control guy saw coming right away and took pains to defuse, saying: "If he survives being orphaned so young, we'll definitely find him a home." Which broke my heart. How could anyone survive all alone at that age?

The Juneau International Airport reported a record-setting 85.06 inches of precipitation the first year we lived on the bus. Juneauites are used to rain, but what were you supposed to do with so much of it?

We rarely had friends over—where would we put them? Tekla and I did our best to amuse each other, but too many rainy days in a row, and it got to feeling like the wet hand of doom had it out for us. Sometimes I could lay in bed all day reading. But on this Saturday, I felt as if I'd levitate off the bed if I kept still one minute longer with that rain drip, drip, dripping on the tin roof above me.

"Let's do something," I said to Tekla. "We could go to the beach?"

She shook her head, frustrated. "The tide's too high."

"Want to see if Mason's shooting hoops down the road?" I wouldn't say Mason considered me a friend. Still, he lived a five-minute walk down the highway, and there were no other kids nearby, so I sometimes went to his place to blow off steam when I got all cooped up and twitchy. Tekla shook her head again, flipping a strawberry blonde braid over her shoulder. I didn't mind, really. I found dribbling a wet basketball as much fun as running full speed at a wall.

We schlepped over to the empty lot next door with a set of badminton rackets we'd found at a yard sale. The lot featured a wide, gravelly U-turn and a pothole as wide and deep as a kiddie pool in the middle. We played without a net, oblivious to the rules, aiming just to keep the birdie aloft.

"Point for me if you drop it!" I said, pounding the plastic shuttlecock right at her, low and fast. Tekla threw out a long arm to volley, danced over the puddle, and dropped her racket in the mud.

"You always make the rules," she said, shaking sludge from her fingers.

I shrugged. "What do you want to do, then?" Not much remained but to crawl home to the Green Machine.

I didn't want to go in. Not ever again. It had gotten so I couldn't breathe on the bus. Without a room to go to and only one foot of headspace between my mattress and the roof, I'd rather be at Lily's in the playroom writing a screenplay. But, if I had to choose, going inside was better than sitting outside in the rain with Tekla in a funk. Except that back on the bus, C.A. had yet another taped baseball game playing on the small black-and-white television, and the Allman Brothers cranked up loud enough we could hear it thirty feet away. Mom had crawled from her bottom bunk that morning to make a cup of coffee before curling back up in bed with a book, saying she needed some space. We'd both asked to stay over at friends' houses, but Mom said to ask C.A. since he had to drive us, and C.A. said no for whatever reason. Given what a pain in the patchouli we were for him, you'd think he'd want to get rid of us for a while.

We still didn't exactly see eye-to-eye on how to spend our time off; us from school, him from work. For instance, when we girls grew bored with life on the bus, C.A. frequently invited us to walk four miles to town to find something to do. In case you're wondering, that's a long piece of road to cover in the rain. I usually looked like a miniature version of Sasquatch by the time I got to town, road grime dripping from everything, even my eyelashes, thanks to the many friendly North Douglas drivers who never stopped to offer me a ride.

If we'd all grown up together, maybe we'd have found some common ground, and I wouldn't have squandered my wishes on milkshakes, heated houses, wrestling matches, and *Star Trek* reruns. Unfortunately, C.A.'s idea of fun was to shout at the Cubs from the middle of our tiny living space while chugging cheap beer.

From my perspective, a person could have more fun sawing off their left hand than watching baseball for any length of time. I once actually tried to do this out of boredom with the rusty old hand saw we used to cut logs for the stove. While I found I couldn't manage to work the blade against my skin hard enough to leave more than a ragged scratch, I did prove beyond the beyond that even the attempt was more exciting than the liveliest baseball game.

I looked up at the sky and sighed. The clouds had bunched up and gone dark, promising more rain. Our oversized raincoats were so threadbare we'd be drenched in seconds when the sky let loose again. We kicked a few pebbles of gravel around before giving up and sitting together on a fallen tree.

I tossed my racket and caught it by the handle. "Why don't you make the rules?" I said, finally. Tekla did a dramatic shoulder-to-ear kind of why not shrug before dragging her racket slowly across the gravel and moving back into position.

If I lost my sister to a bad day, there was nothing left. Sometimes I bullied her until she cried, but twenty minutes later, we'd be screaming and laughing and inventing alternate realities. We were mortal frenemies, which softened the blow of our isolation.

Still, I needed her more than she needed me. Tekla had friends at school. I had Lily and Jeramie and one foot of headspace to live in.

I don't remember what was behind the decision to move on to Marie Drake Middle School for seventh grade. Maybe it was the loneliness. Maybe it was the unceasing rain of that first year on the bus.

At first, I downplayed our living arrangements, making a point of walking toward the ramshackle house on the property rather than the Green Machine when the school bus let us off. But one kid in the back always called out, "Hey, it's your *bus stop*," practically falling out of his seat laughing. Obviously, the secret was out.

I made friends at school in spite of it.

Alexis, with her striped overalls and shoulder-length hair, perpetually tucked up in a knit hat and her ability to make anyone laugh. David, constantly drumming on our shared desk in Geography class and bobbing his head.

But I missed Lily. On lonely days I remembered our quiet ceremony.

A small ceremony. A play ceremony. The way she had said, "*Now we're sisters.*" Like she understood how a person might need more to lean on than my small, scattered family could give. I realized for the first time that a person could make family however they liked. I wondered if anyone else would choose me the way Lily had.

The couple who lived in the house where we parked our bus split up around Christmas of our second year out there. They were desperate enough to get out of the house that they accepted Mom's small savings as down payment. We moved into their place midway through my seventh-grade year, though to call it a house is an overstatement.

It had gotten its start as a one-room fishing shack. Haphazard additions had been made over the years so that one long room now stuck out from the side and a small one poked out by the front door. A square loft had been plopped on top, which was accessible by a drop-down ladder that unfolded into the kitchen. Portions of it had never been sided, and wind blew almost willfully through the cracks. Still, it had a roof and bore some resemblance to a house, and we were off the bus. I leaned hard on grateful thoughts through the coldest nights.

Tekla and I shared the small room by the front door. C.A. built us bunk beds to give us a few feet of walking around space. It felt like a football field compared to my bed on the bus. We hijacked the black-and-white television from the bus after someone gave us an original Nintendo when they upgraded to the new one. After that, we almost never left our room the rest of the school year. I sprawled on the top bunk, Tekla on the bottom, and we played *Super Mario Bros.* and *Donkey Kong* until our eyes were peeled grapes. We listened to Vanessa Williams on eternal repeat because I could only afford a single tape after I spent my summer's festival earnings on our first ever boombox.

"This is so much better than the bus," I said at least once a day for the first six months.

To which Tekla said, "What bus? I don't know what you're talking about."

Memory Cliff

~~~

It's a cowboy-colored day. Too-bright sunlight washes the dry grasses lining the gravel drive from orange to white, dulling the gray pebbles way down below to flat brown. I am little enough to barely notice the scratch of the wood slats on my cheek as I press my face through the rails of the second-story balcony. It is summer in Oregon, and birds are chirping somewhere nearby. It's possible I think I can fly when I let loose the rails, but instead, I drop, boneless as a rag doll, to the rocks below.

My sister says I'm crazy, and she's the one who fell. "That's how I got this scar," Tekla says, jutting out her lower lip. "No, that's how I got *this* scar," I say, pointing at the lump on my own lip. How else would I remember the wind drawing the hair back from my face, forcing my eyes open even as I tried to close them? The way the rocks loomed up at me, little pebbles stretching to boulders as I plummeted. Why would I remember that fall every time I climbed four rungs up a ladder or rode a chairlift or leaned too heavy against the rail at a scenic overlook?

"This baby needs me so much," Mom said when I was very little, clutching a shrieking newborn Tekla as I tried to climb into her lap to help her comfort our fiery new rage machine. "I need you to find something else to do."

As an infant, Tekla rarely had five tear-free minutes at a time. She did screaming hunger fits, week-long crying jags, and fist-pounding growth spurts—throughout which the only place she could sleep was in Mom's arms.

I wanted to sleep in Mom's arms too, but there's only room for one baby. Instead, I dragged a pile of books to the hall where I could just see Mom's back and the riot of legs that was Tekla wailing away. I sat there often, pointing out pictures in my books and telling stories to my Raggedy Anne doll.

Eventually, I found other things to do when Mom had her hands full with Tekla, and then later Camden. I dug up plants to see what their roots looked like and pulled everything I could reach out of the cupboards before tromping through it all like Godzilla. I sometimes wandered over to neighboring houses when no one was looking.

It went like that forever: me finding things to do, one eye always on the lookout for an opening in my mother's arms. Until one day, something flipped, and Tekla crawled into my lap for her bottle. She stayed there for ten years. I was almost never lonely again.

For the first five or six years, Tekla and I wore identical handmade clothes, shared identical toys in different colors, and ate the same meals sunup to sundown. When you're barely fourteen months older than your sister, the only thing you ever do apart is go to separate classes. Of course, we said *yes* when people asked if we were twins, even as Mom shook her head *no*. When they asked, *Did I take very good care of my baby?* I said *yes* to that, too. Caregiver and near-twin. Small wonder, I sometimes forget what happened to which of us. Or when.

I know this memory is not entirely my own because I remember it as Tekla and myself at once, as though we were one body with multiple personalities:

We are driving from our dusty hillside apartment in Pendleton, Oregon, down the long, sloping, dirt road that will take us to church. We are wearing long dresses, and our hair has been flattened into the smoothest, tightest, most headache-inducing ponytails a determined mother can inflict and sprayed into place with Aqua Net. Mom's in the passenger seat wearing a shapeless brown dress and no makeup. Thom's at the wheel laughing at something on the radio, his black mustache stretched wide with a grin.

Our car is a small four-door sedan, the seats blistered and cracked from heat and use. Sunlight slants across the hillside the way it does late in the morning or early in the evening. It is as perfectly Sunday as Sunday can be in these dry hills.

Camden has not yet been born. I am almost four years old, and Tekla is almost three. It's the early 80s, and car seats aren't yet in vogue. Tekla is fiddling with everything in reach: me, the seatbelt, the door handle.

"*No, no, no!*" I say, but Tekla scrunches her button nose up and shoves me off even as her belt buckle silently unlatches, and her door falls open on a rut in the lane. Her expression is a cross between scowl and surprise as she tumbles to the pitted dirt road.

I twist in my seatbelt, trying to look out the window, sobbing. *Sissie, Sissie, Sissie!*

Then I am screaming from the middle of the road, reaching uselessly for the car as it trundles away, mindless as a herd of cattle kicking up a slow trail of dust. I see myself from above like I am a ghost hovering over my own body. I am dusty as a cinnamon donut, smaller than the boulders and scrub brush dotting the hillside. Pebbles are embedded in the skin of my arms, legs, and face. I choke on the grit in my mouth as tears leak in, swishing it all to mud.

The dust has long since settled at the bend in the horizon where my family disappeared before I hear the sound of tires jouncing over potholes once again. The nose of the car jerks back into view, gravel spitting into the air with an urgent tug of the steering wheel.

I *have* fallen out of three moving vehicles, but I never left the rear seat of the car that time. Still, I remember the pain of dry earth caking bloody gashes, curious flies, and the panic of the endless wait on that very particular morning. I know this memory belongs to my sister. Yet, I feel it to be truly mine.

I honestly can't say whether I fell from that particular second-story deck or Tekla did. I have fallen off an absurd number of things in my life: bikes, walls, monkey bars, the top bunk, a skateboard. I've fallen into an ornate splashing water fountain, off at least one second-story deck, and once from the underside of an unfinished stairwell, which I'd thought would be a fun place to practice some sport climbing moves.

I've had three or four serious bell ringers, the last one so bad that twenty years later, I'm not sure I've fully recovered. One day my future neurologist will shake their head in befuddlement (as my chiropractor recently did) and ask, *How did you do this to yourself?*

I suspect that somewhere along the way, my memory of one of those falls linked itself to a family event. A story told over and over until it became *the big fall.* Somehow the memory and the moment cross-wired, and I adopted that specific Falling off the Balcony story as my own.

There is probably an explanation for this confusion of memory—something to explain how children sometimes can't differentiate between their lived experiences and those of their intimates. But since I never misremembered anyone else's experiences but Tekla's, I preferred to think of us as psychic near-twins. Because weren't we?

Either way, I've still got this scar on my lip.

"No, *I'm* President," Tekla said at least thirty times a week when we moved out of the bus and finally had a room of our own again for the first time in years. "You're Scum. You deal."

Beats me how she got excited about card games in the first place. I suspect she stuck with it because she could get away with calling me *scum* or *asshole*. Sometimes she'd even shout *bullshit!* just to see how far she could go, though we usually said *liar* when we absolutely knew adults were in the danger zone.

"Okay. How many do I deal now?" I always had to ask even if she'd just told me the hand before.

I never got the hang of all the rules—which she picked up nearly instantaneously from a book she'd found at the thrift store—and numbers didn't squirrel around on her the way they did for me. I could repeat a string of numbers out loud while simultaneously writing them down and still write them totally out of order. This drove every math teacher I ever had absolutely out of their heads. I hated that the values always changed in card games, like with wild cards or when a two got to be higher than an ace. Tekla instinctively recounted the cards whenever I dealt. I was that unreliable.

We didn't have much in the way of a social life outside of school. Who had the money? And sleepovers, when we could score one, were mostly one way: we went to other people's houses. But only if we could talk someone into staying sober enough to drive us over there and pick us up again later. If we got lucky and C.A. had to work on a Saturday, we girls would climb up into the loft bed he'd built and snuggle down under a dozen or so blankets to read with Mom. The rest of the time, it was Tekla and me, like always, stuck in the bedroom playing Rummy, Speed, and President, complaining all the while. *We never do anything fun.*

Our psychic link broke at some point, and Tekla and I split into separate people with individual stories. I don't suppose we chose which of our shared stories lit up the Things to Remember portion of our minds, but we've somehow taken our joint experiences and shaped different meanings from them. She calls our childhood *unconventional*, where I might choose *unpredictable*, *bohemian*, or *lonesome*. Though, unconventional applies, too.

Then again, Tekla loved Solitaire, while I preferred Memory. Only I called it Twinsies. You paired cards laid face down in an evenly spaced square and flipped two cards over at a time, looking for pairs: two sevens or two fives. I always watched for the aces (Tekla and me) and the queens (Mom) and the jacks (Camden) and tried to match them as quick as I could. That way, if I didn't finish the game with more than half the cards paired on my side, at least I'd liberated my family from the chaos and uncertainty of forgetfulness.

I still shout, "Twinsies!" when I match a pair of aces. *You and me, kid*, I tell my psychic other half. *I'm always looking out for you.* And I feel a little tug in my heart like she's heard me.

Brian and the Brain

~~~

"Do you have enough room?" I whispered over my shoulder.

Tekla wiggled a whole-body nod. We laid back-to-back in one of the twin beds in our room at Grandma's house in Ketchikan, where we'd been since school let out for summer break. We clutched books in front of our faces, pretending to read. We were really just a pair of antennae in knee-length T-shirt pajamas, testing the air for danger.

"You have to quit drinking, C.A.," Mom said. She was on the extension in Grandma's room. Even with the door firmly shut, the hard edge in her voice ghosted through the hallway to our room, the knobby backbone of it standing out. "I can't live like this."

It had been fun in the early days. Bloody Marys before noon on the weekend. Day drinking at festivals. A case of Rainier in the unfinished part of the house that she used as an art studio with a fire blazing in the woodstove while she worked on a project and C.A. watched whatever game was on. I don't know that it ramped up or if something changed in Mom. Either way, the gauntlet had dropped, and that was that.

I kicked off my blanket, shivered, and pulled it back up, uncertainty crackling through me. This was the flash of lightning before rolling thunder shakes your house to the ground. I pressed my spine into Tekla's until she pushed back in acknowledgment. We settled in to wait.

It took a year for the storm to break, by which time I'd stopped looking for it. It blew in fast, quick as a failed heart. And it washed my whole world away.

The first bolt of lightning landed while Mom was in Anchorage with Aunty Jolette, whose father lay dying. Out of five stepdads, Mom only ever had dad feelings for Harry. He'd formally adopted her, given her a sister, a last name, and arms to escape to as a teen when she ran away from home.

Mom had been in Anchorage for months. First the hospital, then hospice, then sorting out the remains of Harry's life. Tekla and I stayed with separate friends most of that time. Because without Mom to run interference with C.A., we'd threatened to run away after the first week.

My classmate Jenny and her lawyer dad, David, took me in. It was just the two of them in a huge house with tons of food and the biggest television I'd ever seen. They lived a short fifteen-minute walk from school. Heaven. And there was Tobias Botkin Lee, his full name so beautiful to my thirteen-year-old mind I couldn't help saying the whole thing. The way he quietly took my hand on a late-night walk with Jenny and a posse of kids. A pause under the glow of a streetlamp. Rain misting our hair. A kiss. Another. A giddy certainty of more to come.

Minutes later, we were on a plane.

Mom had called us home out of the blue. "Pack your things," she said as we walked in the door. We hadn't even known she'd returned.

Lightning.

"What about C.A.?" I said.

"My daddy died. It's time to go," she said simply.

Thunder.

The way I remember it, we packed through the night. We called our closest friends to say goodbye and boarded a plane for Anchorage early on a gray morning, eyes swollen with the shock of it all. Mom says this memory is skewed because it took us three weeks to pack, but I just don't believe it. You can hug your friends goodbye when you have that much time.

I wondered if my father would collect us at the airport in Anchorage. Would I recognize him somehow, with all the years between us? Despite our brief meeting, I barely recalled how tall he was, what kind of clothes he wore, what his house smelled like. Could I love a stranger? Did I have to? I worried I didn't belong in the big city where I was born but had not really ever lived. Or in Dude's life, for that matter.

Mom hunched in the aisle seat like she had recently been unplugged from life support, limp with fatigue and grief and worry. Her hair frizzed out of a knot twisted low on her neck. I had only met Harry once. I remembered that he had ferrets with burning red eyes and an easy manner that Mom tilted into like a post into its beam.

I couldn't fully comprehend my mother's anguish, but I'd had a lot of practice losing half-hearted dads and leaving in the dead of night by then. It gave me a sense of how bad things were for her. I took in the bruises under her eyes, the hurt in her miles-long stare. *This is way worse than the faraway place*, I thought. I'd never seen anything like it in all our years together.

I owned a powerless anger. For all of it. For leaving everything, yet again. For the uncertainty. For the heartbreak at my mother's door.

I slipped my hand into hers and squeezed gently. Then for one moment, a shining glimmer of hope lanced through me. Maybe leaving C.A. meant we could finally get back to being the *peapod*. Long minutes passed before she squeezed back.

Eventually, I licked tears from the corner of my lip and asked, "What are we going to do? Where will we live?"

Mom sighed, shoulders dropping another half-inch. "We're staying with my friend, Brian," she said. "You'll like him. He was at your birth." Which isn't saying much. If half the stories were true, everyone in Anchorage had been at my birth.

It was Brian, not my father, who met us at the airport. He wore a fifteen-year-old tweed sports coat, a golf cap, and brown rayon pants. Tobacco-smoke-stained a brown swath the width of his hooked nose in an otherwise white mustache. His eyes softened at the sight of Mom and the small, frayed worry doll of hope I had carried that we might have her to ourselves for a while unraveled entirely.

We moved into Brian's awkward L-shaped apartment, which required Mom and Brian to walk through the small room Tekla and I shared to reach theirs. Brian, we learned, had been our mother's secret love when I was born. But as a close friend of Dude's, it hadn't worked out back then.

"I couldn't have left Juneau without Brian's help," she told us after Camden arrived for the summer. "You know we had to leave, don't you?"

All three of us kids were lined up on the queen mattress we shared. Camden and I fiddled with our Nintendo controllers. Tekla looked awkwardly at her hands.

We could only mumble and nod. We didn't have a say anyway. It had been hard with C.A., sure, but leaving Juneau seemed like a punishment. And Brian's warm welcome felt like the sticky middle of a spider's web.

What my mother saw in Brian is so far beyond me I can't even look back on him with a generous eye and discover some forgotten trait I hadn't recognized at the time for its greatness. Like C.A., the thing we had most in common was our love for my doe-eyed songbird of a mother. At well over six feet, Brian had wiry black curls that trickled down into a stiff white-black beard, a hawkish nose under thick, harsh eyebrows, and the sallow, sunken cheeks of a man slowly starving to death. How a well-fed man could be so skinny, I've never understood. His duds drooped from his frame with only slightly more animation than they might while hanging from a clothesline.

Though they never married in their thirteen years together, Mom called Brian her husband and encouraged us now and then to call him "dad." Which got a hard pass. I wish I knew then that you can let a person drift on by like air and never even smell them if you choose.

Anchorage is a sprawling city with more people and concrete buildings than all the fishing towns I'd grown up in put together. It left me feeling loose in my skin. The municipality is a wide bowl with the ocean to the west and the Chugach Mountains rising to the east. Half of the state's population lives there, and it's busy in a way that overwhelmed me in those early days. I wasn't used to traffic, or sirens, or a wide swath of industry between my mountains and me.

"If you let me go home, I'll stay with C.A.," I told Mom. "I won't fight him. I promise." I may as well have asked the summer sun to set at noon.

Mom just shook her head, brows doing, *What? Are you crazy?* "I don't want to go back to that life," she said. "All that bickering between you guys. The drinking. The unfinished house."

I knew what she meant. But I imagined a way we could go back and be just us. The way we were supposed to be. We could do it, even without C.A. I just knew it.

"We are not going back," Mom said.

"Actually," Brian said, crossing a leg and laying his lit cigarette in the heavy glass ashtray on the table, "I've got job offers in New Zealand and California."

Brian's choices were between a tribe in New Zealand that needed help with a cultural conflict or studying the mysterious disappearance of the sardine population in the Monterey Bay area. Maybe it was herring. Honestly, I don't remember the specific project that lured him to California or who he worked with. He talked about fish and fishing and pollution and climate change constantly once we got there. Brian called himself a Humanitarian with a capital "H," like a job title. He had neither a legal degree nor certification of any kind. He'd just decided he was the guy who knew the stuff. Whatever his qualifications, he spent countless hours on the phone consulting non-profits and tribes across the globe.

What work he *did* do, he did from home. And I would be surprised if he made any money, given how hard my mother worked to pay their bills despite the crippling depression that fell on her in those years.

"Don't they need humanitarians in Juneau?" I asked lamely, though I already understood that I couldn't make a small town like Juneau big enough to contain my mother during a full life-pivot. My vote only counted in the New Zealand v. California debate. I backed California, where I knew I'd be an Alaskan country mouse without a friend in the world apart from my sister. Still, I could at least fly home for visits in less than a day if I got a job.

We whined. We pleaded. We sulked. We bartered. And still, plans were made, tickets bought. We would move to Monterey the week before school started. I sometimes wonder what I missed in New Zealand.

With a month of summer left before the end of the world, we kids grew listless. Summers had always been ferry season. Cruising up and down the Inside Passage to visit family and camp at festivals.

We became impossibly bored in our shared bedroom and were ecstatic when a couple of rusty old bikes turned up. Several small dirt hills populated the foot trail near Brian's apartment, making for great jumps. One, in particular, drew us back over and over.

The hill curved up just at the end of the trail, where dirt faded to paved parking lot, which was perfect for landing because pavement doesn't spit you sideways on a hard brake the way dirt does. I like to recall the jump as soaring five feet high, but it was probably barely more than a three-footer. Size didn't matter so much to me as long as I could catch air. I took that jump at least a hundred and fifty times until one time, without warning, my chain fell off mid-air. When I tried to plant my feet on the pedals for stability, they simply spun off into air, yanking me sideways. My head hit the pavement so hard it bounced.

I can still hear the wet smack of my skull meeting blacktop, the bike crashing on top of me, and Camden's far-off voice floating toward me. "Keema! Shit. Keema, wake up!" He was a few months shy of ten.

I don't know how he got me home. After that, everything went black.

When my brain turns back on in that moment, I'm somehow sitting in Brian's apartment, and he's checking the dilation of my pupils, and I'm thinking someone should make it, like, a law or something that you have to buy your kids helmets. There's a ringing in my ears so angry and loud that I can't make out what Brian is saying in his monotonous, know-it-all voice, but I do notice his cigarette slowly burning itself out on the table beside him.

My brain and my body have dislocated. If I think hard, I can make my hands move. But I can't feel them. I can't feel anything except this pulsing bolt of electricity surging through me, and I think maybe it could be my soul, if souls are liable to catch fire. I think I must be dying, and the burning-stabbing sensation is my sinner's soul getting slowly sucked into hell for being such a lousy kid: I'm selfish and lazy and funny looking and jealous of normal people. Whoever they are. No one even likes me or wants me. That's why Mom loves Tekla best. That's probably the real reason my father left. Thom remarried and had his own kids. C.A. had probably hated me from the start. I don't trust this Brian guy, either, but Mom seems to think he's made of angel song. Too bad for all of them because I'm dying now, and we'll never fix any of it.

There aren't words to describe the terror I felt in the throes of my first anxiety attack. Or any of the rest of them, for that matter. They lasted for ten years. Ten years where I never heard the term traumatic brain injury or that TBI's can kick off anxiety disorders. Even now, it's hard to recall the harrowing half out-of-body/half paralysis they brought without a jolt of adrenaline arcing up my spine.

Suddenly, everything frightened me: food and medicine, my heartbeat, anything that could result in a fall, and all new things in general. My eyes seemed permanently set to dilated: all pupil, all the time.

Everywhere I went, I felt death pressing in on me: in bed, at the grocery store, on the bus. The walls of my classrooms sometimes melted, the floor tipping away like a poorly wrought copy of an M.C. Escher painting. I developed a hypochondriac's aches and pains and allergies, none of which I'd had before. I struggled to eat and refused to do anything that might set off an attack.

Since Brian's very favorite thing in the world was to pace around the living room while chain-smoking and issuing authoritative prescriptions about things that were none of his business, I became his new favorite target.

"The reason you're having so much anxiety is that the trauma from your childhood is resurfacing," he'd say, staring down at me on the couch. I had no interest in these sessions, never mind the fact that he had access to my personal history, which I had not elected to share with him. I occupied my field of vision by rolling an endless supply of flawless cigarettes out of the tin of Drum rather than look back up at him.

Mom thought maybe I should see a doctor for once, but Brian waved her off. "It's teen angst," he told her. "She's a bundle of traumas in a teenager's body. She's just being dramatic." Said the guy who claimed to have walking pneumonia that he'd acquired when the government tested a mystery insecticide in the mountains where he'd been backpacking twenty years before. I suspected his poor health might have more to do with a ceaseless smoking habit and a touch of hypochondria himself. Or maybe I was just being dramatic.

I was a different person when we boarded the plane for California than I had been a few months earlier when we left Juneau. I didn't know that a head injury can cause a person to feel like they don't have a body or worry that they have suddenly developed mental illness. By then, I'd begun to believe it when Brian said I was so ruined by Ray that I didn't have a hope of normalcy, or fitting in, or getting over it, or really ever being *okay* if I didn't confront a childhood trauma that had absolutely nothing to do with the pain in my head. I saw his point, but I didn't have enough experience to back up my certainty that this was *not* about Ray.

I needed a doctor, but I got Know-it-All-Brian. So sure of his diagnosis, you'd believe him if you saw him on a daytime talk show. To the best of my knowledge, he didn't have a Psychology degree, either.

Tekla only recalls a few odd moments from that time. Once, I leapt from the table in the middle of dinner at a friend's house and ran home without saying a word to anyone. Sometimes I paced while slapping my arms and talking out loud, trying to convince myself I was real. Other than that, she missed the whole thing. What a weirdo I must have been before the anxiety attacks.

I barely slept in the first year, and then only if I held Tekla's sleeping hand. Her hand I could feel. When I pinched myself, I couldn't feel the press of my own fingers doing the pinching. The pain came through from far away, like a memory. But Tekla was as real and solid and reliable as a grilled cheese sandwich on an empty belly. The whole of me might have been a ghost, but my sister's hand in mine kept the wind from blowing me away.

Smoking

~~~

My mother went to bed and didn't get up for half a year after the move to California. She'd lost her dad and left her home, her friends, and everything she knew and loved. Grief turned her inward, emptied the vaults she'd so carefully stockpiled since escaping home. It shone a light into the dark corners she'd been careful to avoid for so long.

She ventured out of her room about a month after she'd gone to bed. She called Tekla and me out to the double wide's shabby living room. Brian brought her a cup of coffee and set the tin of Drum beside her on our tattered couch.

"I've told you before . . ." Mom said. She paused to flick her lighter, inhale, and pull a loose thread of tobacco from her lip. "I've told you that my brother Buck was a bad man." She looked like a person recently freed from a medieval dungeon. Bone thin, limp-haired; nearly caved in. It was the first time I truly saw the graveyard my mother had been carrying around inside her. "But there's so much more to it than that," she said. She absently rubbed the lighter with her thumb like a prayer bead.

I would spare you my mother's story if I could since it is not my story to tell anyway. But you must know that the single most salient part of my mother's young life was this: she was raped by her oldest brother for many, many years.

Her brother Neal tried it first, whispering naked into her room one night after the house had gone quiet.

"What are you doing?" she murmured sleepily when he slid under the blankets with her. He was reed-thin and short, not much older than her.

"I thought we could play," he said, tickling her awake.

"What?" she shoved his hands away. "Why are you naked?"

"Don't you like being tickled? You could get naked, too."

"Gross," she said, pushing him with her fists and feet until he fell out of bed with a thump loud enough to wake the house.

"Okay," he said, throwing out his hands placatingly, afraid someone would come check on the noise. "Okay." He slunk out the door.

But the next night, he came back.

He crept in again, naked as a shelled peanut. This time she kicked free of him and bolted to the door yelling. "Mom! Neal keeps coming into my room naked and messing with me! Make him stop!"

Grandma threw open the door and took in her naked son and her daughter's rumpled nightdress. She gasped. "Why are you tempting your brother with your body?" she slapped my mother's little face hard enough to leave her ears ringing.

"I didn't!" my mother cried, clutching her face. She fled from the angry swats on her back and legs to curl up on the bed.

"And *you*," Grandma rounded on Neal, slapping his face, chest, back, anything she could reach while he hunched in a ball. "There are," *slap*, "no," *slap*, "nasty boys in this family." She raged on, eventually dragging him from the room by his hair.

When Buck started in on my mother a short time later, she knew there would be no saving her. A nine-year-old girl, half the size of her oldest brother. Entirely convinced it was her fault. She could take a beating and the blame if she told Grandma, or she could endure it silently.

Grandma swears still that she never knew, which leaves me to wonder at the mind's ability to white out what it doesn't want to see.

Only after Harry's death did Mom tell Grandma the whole truth. Grandma wouldn't hear it. She couldn't believe her darling, her oldest and strongest, could have harmed his little sister. She was shocked, *shocked, I say*, that my mother blamed her for leaving the kids alone on the homestead where Buck had complete dominion.

"He did *not* own a set of brass knuckles. I would have known. I'm his mother," she would say in one breath. And, "Why didn't you tell me? I'd have beat him black and blue," with the next.

When Aunty Jolette heard this story shortly after Grandpa Harry's funeral, she split wide open until she was just a broken sob on the other end of the couch. "Me too, sister," she said. "Me too." It nailed my mother to the ground.

Aunty Jolette's story and the grief of losing Harry had become too much. She gripped her stomach unconsciously while she spoke, as though trying to keep her insides from spilling out. I wanted to reach across the couch and hold her hand, but her anger bound Tekla and me to our seats.

"I never *imagined* Buck would hurt Jolette, too," Mom said. "She was a *baby*. Who would have thought?" In an era of denial and victim-shaming, they'd grown up believing themselves alone in their suffering, unaware of each other's misery.

One time, Grandma found Jolette, a small, innocent, tortured child around five, washing herself in the bathroom moments after Buck had left her. Grandma thought Jolette was playing with herself and, horrified, belted her for being a dirty little girl. Mom remembers the beating, remembers Jolette's sobs, remembers her own horror at Grandma's puritanical rage. But she had never known the whole truth of her baby sister's torment.

In all my years since Ray, I have never been alone with the shadow of him. There was no secret to the shape of his destruction, no shame, no hiding. My mother and my aunt were silenced equally by their brother's fists and the fear of their mother's recriminations.

Hardest to understand for me was this: Mom had survived well enough without succumbing to a nervous breakdown before Brian showed up. I didn't know yet that trauma has a timeline of its own, so I assumed Brian had talked her into it. I could already see that it worked to his advantage to keep her soft and malleable.

When she wondered out loud if maybe she should call Grandma and talk things out, Brian said, "Your mother did this to you. She oppressed you, manipulated you, beat you, and now denies the abuse you suffered from your brothers. Now it's all bubbling up to the surface, demanding your attention."

Lean into it, he said, or you will never be free.

Brian bathed her sorrow and fed her anger, convinced her that only he could ever comfort her again. She had no will to resist, nor even the desire to. She'd been treading water for so long she felt she couldn't go on anymore. She needed to float for a while. With a sigh, she shored up against the island Brian built for her.

When we did see her in those early months, our mother seemed smaller, hollowed out, and crumpled. She lived in the faraway place now. When we complained that Brian wouldn't let us in to see her, she said, "It's just for right now. He wants to give me time to process. It's not the worst thing, is it?"

Of course, it *was* the worst thing for us. We didn't even know the guy she left us with when she went inward. But who were we to say?

Brian didn't let Grandma through either. She called every Sunday, as she'd done all my life. Brian made excuses. Mom was working. Mom was painting. Mom was in the shower. Eventually, he said, "She doesn't want to talk to you," and hung up the phone. After that, I had to find things to do out of the house on Sundays because Grandma started asking for *me*.

Soon Brian made sure we girls couldn't get in to see Mom when she was home at all. He kept her tucked away in their back bedroom with the door locked. I could hear her great, wracking sobs clear on the other end of the trailer. It made me want to break things just so I could fix them and give her a smile with my skill.

I felt sure we could comfort her in some way. We always had before. But Brian snarled, "Leave her alone!" when we snuck past him to try to knock on her door. You had to plead a good case to gain an audience with her, and it had to be completely undeniable, like a school form that needed signing or a report card.

"I don't see where you get to decide if we can see our mom or not," I said when he sent Tekla crying to her room for knocking on Mom's door.

"Well that's too bad," he said. "Because she doesn't want to see you or hear your sniveling. She has enough heartache without you adding to it."

Part of me didn't believe him. She might have been remote at times, but even stoned and absorbed in a book, she'd always loved to have us next to her on the couch where she could reach out and rub her thumb across our foreheads now and then. Still, another part of me believed I was a burden to my mother, what with the constant anxiety I had now. My endless resistance to Brian's authority. The way I begged every day to go home to Alaska. The sorrows at her door I couldn't even fully comprehend.

Finally, the part of me that had never found a way back into my mother's arms won out, and I didn't fight as hard to get in to see her anymore.

"What are you doing here, sugar bear?" Mom said, surprise and pleasure crinkling at the corner of her eyes. I'd walked the fifteen minutes from Monterey High down to Fisherman's Wharf to find her. She'd set up shop with an easel and a couple of tall collapsible director's chairs to do quick-sketch portraits. She wore roughly thirty-five layers of clothes and kept a thermos of hot coffee beside her all day because the thing about Monterey is that it's damp.

While the fog usually lifts by noon, the way I remember it, the air remains heavy and wet most of the year.

"I miss you," I said. I didn't say, *Brian can't keep us apart forever.*

Her face rose so small and serious from her winter shroud she might have been sporting a shrunken head. I ached to hold her, to lean into her with my whole heart, but I refrained. I'd begun to feel an interloper in her story, so I mostly kept myself to myself whenever I stopped by.

With every visit, I hoped that maybe this time I'd reach in and find her there, reaching back. Instead, she'd talk about spirit walking and reincarnation, how we'd been through past lives together, a mother and daughter duo of endless iterations. It made her happy, even if it left me with questions.

"I miss you, too," she said. "Sit down. How was rehearsal?" I'd gotten a role in the school's production of *Into the Woods.*

"Mr. Welch is crazy mad that I dyed my hair," I said, tugging at the blue streaks in my shoulder-length bob, laughing a little. "He said, 'You're supposed to be Little *Red* Riding Hood, not Little *Blue* Riding Hood.'"

Mom looked up from her easel, taking in the angle of my jaw, dragging an oil pastel crayon across the page without looking. We dropped wordlessly into place out of habit: she with her colors and questions, me with my stories.

"Hmmm," Mom said. "He told me the other night that you should pursue acting." She'd recently had to pick me up from a late rehearsal on her way home because the busses weren't running, and none of my friends could drop me off. "He says you're a natural." The pride in her voice drifted through me like a warm July wind.

The azure waters and soft sand of Monterey Bay over her shoulder offered a warmth and friendliness unlike the gnashing shorelines of my youth. I sat for a few minutes, soaking it in while her hands passed over the easel. Sea lions barked from the docks below and seagulls spun lazy loops above us in the breeze, shrieking gleefully.

A woman sauntered up to look over Mom's shoulder. "Wow!" she said.

"This is my daughter," Mom said. "Isn't she gorgeous?"

The woman nodded. "Can you do me?"

"I have to get back for the next act anyway," I said, sliding from the folding chair. "I love you." I kissed my mother's cheek, breathing in coffee and sandalwood and the warmth of her body wafting up from all those layers of wool. I wanted more. More time. More good moments. More of us.

Mom turned the sketch so I could see it: blue eyes, pointy nose, round chin, red hair with blue in it. There I was. The daughter she loved. That paper girl wasn't a mess of anxiety and confusion, loneliness and hurt. I wondered if I would ever be that girl again.

I rolled enough cigarettes for Brian, it seemed only natural when I finally started smoking. It calmed the anxiety some. The tin of Drum was a primary feature in the landscape of our living room and usually not hard to find. Sometimes it wandered into Mom and Brian's room, so I'd stock a sandwich bag with tobacco and rolling papers now and then.

On one occasion, Brian was out, and Mom had cried herself to sleep in the back room, but the tobacco was nowhere to be found. I tapped on her door. No answer.

"Mom?" No answer. I sighed. The way she could sleep now, she'd be in there until the next afternoon.

I turned the knob. Locked. Standard practice when she was smoking weed, to keep up the facade that we didn't know what she was doing in there. She'd probably forgotten to unlock it before falling asleep.

"*Honestly*. What if there was an emergency?" I muttered, taking a butter knife to the lock. I crept in quietly. Mom was nearly invisible in a tangle of heavy blankets. The room smelled of stale smoke and sleep. Afternoon light drifted through a crack in the handmade curtains to caress her cheek. I ached to be near her. Back in Juneau, I might have brought in a book and curled up next to her, but Brian would have an out-of-body experience if I tried that now.

I snagged the tobacco tin and peeled up the lid, figuring I'd take what I needed and leave the tin so she wouldn't have to search for it when she woke up. The seal released with a faint pop as the lid came free, louder than I had expected. Mom rolled over, startled. Confusion and sleep drew her eyes into a squint.

"What are you doing?" she said, befuddled.

"I needed tobacco," I said.

"Why do you have a knife?" Her eyes were wild and unfocused. I couldn't tell if she knew me. I hadn't seen that look before. I didn't know it for the panic of a trauma survivor roused by surprise.

I only looked at the butter knife and shrugged. "The door was locked, and you didn't answer."

It hadn't felt like a crossed line until a week later when Brian dragged me into the living room, yet again, for our weekly session on my failure to thrive while he paced and stroked his mustache. He had a whole new glint in his eyes this time.

"You've finally done it," he said. I would swear there was glee in his voice. "You've scared your mother so much she's afraid of you."

"Afraid of *me*?" I glared up at him from the couch.

"You're out all hours," he said. "You refuse to listen to me. And now you've broken into our room and waved a knife in her face."

"Waived *a knife* in her face? You are seriously mentally deficient."

"You broke into our room, right?"

I nodded.

"With a knife, right?"

"A *butter* knife," I said. "I needed tobacco. I would never waive a knife at Mom."

Mom came out of the room with a face so blank it shook me. She cleared her throat and sat on the opposite end of the couch, straight-backed and hard.

"You don't admit it," she said, "but I know you blame me for all this misery. I can't just sit around waiting for you to do something dangerous."

Actually, when I wasn't staving off undiagnosed panic attacks, all I had energy left for was lonesomeness. I'd made friends. I went to school every day and passed my classes. But I still pined for the life we could have if we had Mom to ourselves.

I owned a homesickness for something small and warm I couldn't even remember, let alone name. I didn't know how to hold it. So we used the wrong words for the right problem. Brian saying, "Your anger is unhealthy for your mother." And Mom saying, "Clearly you think you can do a better job taking care of yourself than we can, the way you're out with your theater friends all the time." Her dark eyes were as hard and unforgiving as petrified wood. In almost the same breath, she said, "You've been weird and clingy lately, too. And I think you have a crush on me. It's a Freudian thing. Perfectly natural, but I don't think it's healthy to let it go on like this." She spoke, but Brian's words fell out of her mouth.

I blame her susceptibility to that idea on her general mental fog at the time because no kind of examination can make sense of it. And when I asked her about it years later, she couldn't believe her own words. "I said that?" she said. And then, "Brian could convince an unfertilized egg to hatch in the refrigerator."

"I called Thom," Mom said then. "He'll take you in. So, you can go back to Sitka, or you can go to Anchorage and live with your older brother Zach." Deals had been struck, and me the last to know. Thom had a new family, though. Whenever I'd visited lately, I felt myself hemmed in by busy work and shirts tucked in and God. Compared to that, Zach was a relative unknown, but at least he had some weirdness I could relate to. A girl like me could find herself better somewhere a little weird.

I didn't have wind enough to get up a sail and navigate toward safer waters. I sat pinned to the couch, drenching the cigarettes I rolled until each one crumbled into tiny piles of tear-soaked tobacco and flecks of soggy paper in my hands. I was fourteen years old and halfway through my freshman year in high school. And now: proof. There was no way back to my mother.

I wished for the strength to live up to the drama of the moment. What would a delinquent do? Slash a few of Mom's canvasses? Punch a hole in the fake wood paneling?

I owned no such anger. Only weariness. How long do you try to talk a tornado into taking a deep breath before you duck and cover? I fought the urge to curl into the couch and sleep. I worried that if I closed my eyes, I would disintegrate as easily as the rolling papers in my hands.

Discrepancies

~_~_~

Pretend I am The Ghost of Children Grown, and I am haunting my mother as she breathes through another contraction. Sweat stands at her brow, inspired in equal parts by wonder and worry. I am close to emerging into her world of tarot cards, fairy caves, music, and artistic poverty.

I have imagined this scene a thousand times. Always, I hover in the doorway of her small bedroom in the trailer, elbowing the occasional drunk partygoer out of the way, trying to get through to her.

"Mom. Listen. You need to get me a birth certificate right away, okay? Don't wait three years. You have no idea how hard it is to get a copy of a delayed birth certificate from the State of Alaska."

She is making an anxious loop: bed, hallway, toilet. Her round belly is so firm it practically vibrates with each contraction. She can't hear me.

"It's my birthday," I say. "You should write it down somewhere. It'll come in handy. For legal documents, you know?" In the small yard outside, someone passes a joint to my father. He pushes his lips out into a tiny "o" to suck in the smoke and laughs. But even as a ghost, I can't pin down the sound of his laugh because, in real life, it is too vague and unfocused for me to recall from our little time together.

"I know it doesn't seem like a big deal to you today," I tell my mother, "but in seven years or so, it'll really annoy you when you can't remember for sure what day I was born." My mother is so young. Three months past her twentieth birthday. Her long, dark hair curtains a smoothly innocent and radiantly freckled face. She has not yet raised three kids. She's never met Ray.

Sadly, my mother is no Ebenezer Scrooge. And my imaginary incorporeal self is far less persuasive than those time-traveling ghosts of his. I can't show her the social security card with what looks suspiciously like a kindergarten-era signature and say, "Isn't this neat? It's got the wrong last name on it because I didn't know Dude put his name on my birth certificate until I got a copy of it when I was sixteen."

I can't tell her that I think she is brave and wonderful to birth us kids at home and that her sweet, low voice will always land on me like sunshine after too many long, dark, winter days. Or that no matter how much she wants to raise us off the grid, it's virtually impossible unless you go all the way and join some kind of backwoods commune. Even in Alaska, you need birth certificates and vaccination records to enter public school or find gainful employment.

No fantasy can change the fact that the details of my birth were somewhat fuzzy by the time she got around to getting our birth certificates. She'd simply picked a date for me in a hurry that sounded close enough. A date that was, inexplicably, one day earlier than the day we celebrated for the next sixteen years. I only figured this out when my friend Alexis and her mother helped me get my documents together so I could apply for a driver's license.

All that time, my social security card said one thing, my birth certificate said another, we celebrated a questionable birthday, and I'd had a whole extra last name without even knowing.

The whole moving-in thing started with a haircut. It began innocently enough, with a pair of two-inch sewing scissors. Alexis usually applied these to the split ends of her own hair, which fell to her butt on the rare occasion when she removed the knit Rasta cap she lived in. I had shoulder-length hair at the time, with streaks of blue that framed my face.

"You have school all day, work all night, homework, The Lost Abbey on the weekends. How long can you keep this up?" Alexis asked as she worked. I'd been living with my older brother Zach for almost a year, bussing across Anchorage at 6 a.m. to attend West Anchorage High School, then bussing back across town to work the closing shift at the hot dog stand outside of Eagle Hardware. After close, I walked two miles home to my apartment behind the Taco Bell on Tudor Road. Most nights, I couldn't start on my homework before 11 p.m.

I'd had Alexis over to my apartment for a sleepover a few weeks earlier. I'm not sure what she'd thought my home life was like. I doubt her imagination ran as far as the sparse one-room unit I shared with my older brother, dingy with smoke stains and take-out wrappers. Our refrigerator held only condiments, beer, and the congealed leftovers of the pintos-and-cheese cup I ate most nights from Taco Bell because it was close. And after rent, I could only afford to spend sixty cents on dinner. Zach worked nights while I had school and work during the day. We shared the bed in shifts, rarely crossing paths. At twenty-eight, he had virtually no experience with teenage girls anyway.

That night I'd dragged Alexis to the Lost Abbey, an all-ages dance club conveniently located behind my apartment building. On our way in, I said *hey* to the guy with the spiked choke collar smoking out front. I fist-bumped a girl I knew in dayglow jewelry and a pink mohawk who wanted to be a deejay, and stopped to hug a couple of sweet boys holding hands by the stage. We sidled up to the bar, and I splurged on a pop to share with my guest. The single social rule enforced at the club was the age limit for alcohol.

I had some friends among the troublemakers and drunks but felt no pull toward harder days myself. My normal already felt like an involuntary acid trip thanks to the anxiety attacks. I never could get excited about chasing random highs. What drew me to the club was the loud music, the dark dance floor, and the crush of bodies. All of it just enough to make me forget whether I'd had dinner or could afford rent this month.

The Abbey brought Alexis no such comfort. If the sight of my apartment had tripped alarm bells in her mind, the Abbey sent her into full-blown flight. I had no rules to break. It didn't occur to me that I might be pushing the boundaries of what she felt comfortable with. She called her mom for a ride home before we finished our pop, saying cheerfully, "You stay. Have fun. I'll call you tomorrow."

I want to say I talked her into staying. That we walked back to my place and spent the night telling scary stories and crushing over girls and boys like normal teenagers. Instead, I went home alone hours later, without the one true friend I had in all of Anchorage.

"I don't really mind it," I shrugged as Alexis snipped at the nape of my neck with her absurdly small scissors. "It's just . . . this is the way it is."

"We're *fifteen*," she said, straightening my head so that I looked into her small, serious eyes, perched above mine in our reflection. "We're not supposed to be worried about rent, or food, or, like, whether some drunk friend of our brother's is going to go nuts on a coke binge and try to knock down our door because he's feel-ing *friendly*." This event had, in fact, transpired not long before, to my amusement. "You should move in with us," she said decisively, ignoring the skeptical look I gave her.

I'd first met Alexis back in Juneau when she'd stopped me at the Folk Festival to tell me she'd loved watching Tekla and I perform our first set as The Little Rascals. Two years later, we'd been in the same seventh and eighth-grade classes at Marie Drake Middle School. When we left Juneau, I thought for sure I'd never see her again, so it felt like some kind of fate when I found out that she'd moved back to Anchorage shortly before I did. I only paused long enough to make sure the city bus could get me across town before enrolling at her high school. I lived so far outside of her district it was an hour-long commute by bus, but worth it. Now she and her parents, Malcolm and Cindy Roberts were back in their thunderous large house in one of the oldest neighborhoods in town, only a mile or so from where I was born. Malcolm worked as assistant to former Governor Wally Hickel. Cindy had been Mrs. America in 1978 and had a degree in Physical Geography, which she employed tackling various projects around the state. They were *normal, normal, normal* in a way I felt I never could be.

"By the way, how do you feel about a bob?" Alexis interrupted my thoughts.

"Do it!" I said. The bob sounded like an adventure. But moving in made me nervous. I chewed at a hangnail on my thumb. I had the kind of freedom kids my age dreamed about. Who was there to set a curfew? Harass me about school assignments? Force me into regular family dinners or church?

"What's a few rules compared to regular meals?" Alexis countered. By then, we were brushing bits of fine, red hair off our clothes onto the small pile gathering on the carpet, and the bob was nearly done.

Alexis is an artist. Give her a paintbrush and a flat surface, and she will exhale mountains and flowers, shadows, colors, people: life. She is no less an artist with scissors. With her hands in my hair, I felt the world both bigger and simpler than I'd known it to be. Under her gaze, I became a stretched canvas, the future unfixed. She saw in me some kind of something that made her want to give me her own eyes, the better to see myself. I couldn't stand for it to end. After the bob, we moved on to a pixie cut. Then a mullet, a mohawk, and by the time we finally landed on bald, I'd come around to thinking moving in might not be so bad. It would take several months to convince me, but I'd be moved in by Thanksgiving of my sophomore year.

Malcolm clutched a hand to his heart when we traipsed downstairs the next morning. He carefully set his coffee cup down and leaned one hip into the kitchen counter. "Did Alexis do that?" he said.

I ran a hand over the smooth skin of my scalp. "Isn't it amazing?"

"Part of me feels like I'm an imaginary person," I confessed to Cindy when my birth certificate arrived the next spring with its great revelations. She had helped me file for it months earlier. "I don't even have an actual birthday."

We were sitting on the short flight of wide, carpeted steps in the foyer that led up to the living room and kitchen. If you tally up the hundreds of hours we've bent our heads in conversation, the bulk of them happened right there on those vast, white stairs.

Cindy wrapped one arm around my shoulders and held my hand with the other. Her nails were naturally long and painted in a barely-there nude color; perfectly smooth and round. "You just have to remember the way your mother loves you is special all on its own, darlin'," she said. To this day, she calls me darlin', like an extra middle name. *Keema Darlin'*, she says on a delighted breath whenever I call.

Malcolm and Cindy had welcomed me into their family like a long-lost, redheaded love child. A possibility that Cindy's mother never fully gave up on. "Are you sure you didn't step out on Malcolm?" she had asked Cindy with a wink the first time she laid eyes on me. Given that I am either twenty-two or twenty-three days older than Alexis and that I lack the regal chin and characteristic Roberts family smile, I thought it pretty obvious Alexis and I weren't near-twins the way you could confuse Tekla and me. Still, I called them mom and dad and sister, and they introduced me to friends as their kid. I can't remember sleeping more than four or five hours a night in all my time in Anchorage before I moved in with them.

For ten months, Cindy held my hand when I broke to pieces at night for missing my mother or when anxiety attacks overwhelmed every cell in my body and left me shivering on my bed in the guest room. She looked past baggy clothes and piercings, my shaved head, and my tendency to chatter like a squirrel on amphetamines. It was Cindy who drove me to the DMV in her fire-engine red GEO Storm and sat in the waiting room while I first presented myself and my several bizarrely inconsistent documents in the hopes of acquiring a driver's license.

"How do you explain these discrepancies?" the teller had asked. She took in my social security card with one name, a birth certificate with another, and school records with the wrong birth date. I rocked back and forth on my heels in the yellow office. The fluorescent lights cast a sickly green pall over my pale hands as I gripped the few pitiful documents that declared me a real, live person.

I wanted to say, *Doesn't everyone have an extra last name and two birthdays?* Instead, I said, "Hippies," and gave the lady an apologetic shrug.

I flashed Cindy my shiny new license afterward, and she drew me into a hug. "Congratulations," she said. "Let's take you out for a drive."

Bewildered as she may have been by the inexplicably winding road that brought me to her door, Cindy never said a thing about my mother's parenting. I loved her all the more for the freedom she gave me to love my mother unconditionally while I struggled to make sense of the space between us.

"What if neither of these days is my real birthday?" I asked as we sat on the stairs taking in my birth certificate. I was aiming for curious but landed somewhere closer to plaintive whine. Cindy could only shrug.

"Shoot," my mother said when I called her that evening. "Really?" She laughed. I could almost see her wide eyes, her mouth drawn sideways in embarrassment. "I'm sorry, honey. I was so flustered when I applied for your birth certificate. I don't even know what date I wrote down. You know how I am with numbers." I couldn't fault her for that. I struggled with numbers in the same way. Still, I needed to know.

"Which do you *think* is the actual date then?"

"Well . . ." she said, and everything I'd learned from our growing-up-together years said the rest.

"Are you even sure which year I was born?"

"Well . . ." she said again. Next, she'd tell me Tekla was actually the oldest, and I'd been hatched from an egg in a baby factory on the Moon.

What followed, though, was a long pause and a faltering breath. Then she said, "I miss you," for all the world like I'd just gone on vacation. The air went out of my lungs, and sudden tears tangled up my throat so I could only gulp in response. "What do you think about coming home?" she said then, her voice whisper-soft and tentative.

I gripped the phone so tightly I could feel my pulse vibrating through it as if my heart would speak what my mouth could not. *Please, please, please.*

I thought about Brian, with his tobacco-stained mustache and penchant for making himself out to be the sanest holier-than-thou self-prescribed therapist the world had ever seen. I thought of Tekla. I'd left midway through her eighth-grade year. She'd be starting her sophomore year in high school soon. I thought of my mother, so young when she had me. She couldn't have guessed at the trouble we'd face together. Maybe I could give Brian another shot if it meant getting my mother back.

Kim Rich stopped in to say goodbye before I left. She lived two houses down and across the street from the Roberts. We'd first met shortly after I moved in. She'd stared at me as we shook hands, rolling my name around in her mouth awhile. A stray brown curl clung to her cheek as she nodded her head thoughtfully. "*Waterfield*," she said, practically in italics. She wore oval glasses and a touch of red on wide, thin lips. "You're not Fawn's daughter, are you?" she asked.

When I nodded *yes*, she'd dragged me in on a one-armed hug and beamed. "I was at your birth," she said. Here she was sixteen years later: the friend of a friend of a future stepdad who'd saved my newborn life. I'd met several people who'd been at the party-that-was-my birth since moving back to Anchorage. Mostly during rare visits to my father's house on getting-to-know-you expeditions. I don't recall meeting anyone who'd been sober during the party besides Kim, though. I ached to know everything about it. "It really was a very beautiful thing," she told me. And crazy. And rowdy.

I thought maybe she could solve the mystery of my birth date, but she only shook her head as we said our goodbyes. "But if you'd seen the way your mother held you, the way you two couldn't take your eyes off each other, you'd know why she wasn't thinking about what day it was or who was too baked to stand upright. Her whole world was you."

After I finished packing, I lined up my unruly documents on the bed like a string of naughty ducklings. I shook my head at them. Social security card, school records, birth certificate, license, none of them matched entirely. Alexis took in my birth certificate and threw an arm around my neck.

"Look at it this way," she said philosophically, "you've got two days to choose from. You could celebrate both of them. Or, like, pick the one you want." Which I did. Now there's one day I use on legal documents, and another day I call my own. Maybe neither of them is my actual birthday. I'll never know.

I thought about the phone call when Mom had asked me to come home. "You are a nut," I'd told her. "I never wanted to leave in the first place."

Mom had laughed that low-in-the-throat laugh that makes you want to laugh right back. "Yeah," she'd said, "but I'm *your* nut."

It's true. In all the years I had wished for new clothes, a permanent place to call home, or the chance to grow up a musical genius without trying, I never wished for another mother. I wanted the one I had. The one who'd invited everyone she knew into her trailer on the day of my birth to welcome me into the world.

"I should go, right?" I asked Alexis.

It hadn't ever occurred to me that I might return to California. The suddenness of leaving this sweet new family I'd made left me feeling untethered.

Alexis had shaped more than my hair with those scissors of hers. She had pulled me into the warmth of her home and loved me unflinchingly. She'd pared back the layers of doubt to reveal a confidence I'd never thought to own.

"Brian is *wrong*," she'd said fiercely whenever I wondered if maybe he'd been onto something, that I could only ever look forward to a life of ruin. "You're not broken. You're *hurt*." I'd begun to believe her, but it was a weak and wingless new feeling. I worried at testing it so soon. Still, a powerful ache drew me back to my mother-like siren song.

I longed to stay. I longed to leave.

Alexis pursed her lips, nodding thoughtfully. "If you don't go, I think you'll always wonder if you should have."

I sighed, wishing I could sleep for a month first.

Alexis ruffled my short hair and smiled. "One last haircut before you go."

All the Way Home

~~~

I expected tears, but the sight of my young mother through the sliding doors at the San Jose International Airport laid a calm over me as steady as if she'd reached out and stroked the hair back from my forehead. Thirty-six and trim, she stood near the baggage carousel with her hands clasped behind her back and one foot thrust forward as though she'd paused mid-stride. She wore a deep blue cardigan with a brightly colored silk scarf knotted at her neck. Her raven hair fell freely over one shoulder, and her lips were fixed in a wide smile that I knew like my own heartbeat. The doors shushed open, and we locked eyes.

The world inhaled.

Overhead announcements muted and the passengers filing into baggage claim stilled. An invisible force propelled me through the void between us until I stood speechless before my mother. We shared a stunned getting-to-know-you-again moment, lost time unfurling over us so that we blended and blurred, past selves settling into new.

Grief had aged her, pressing new wrinkles to her forehead. But her wide brown eyes shone with a hopefulness that hadn't been there when I left.

She seemed somehow smaller than I remembered. Petite. Shy. Timid, even. She stood apart from the crowd, a lifelong outsider past the point of looking for a way in. Had she always been so delicate?

The way my mother looked at me, I might have been a fresh brewed cup of coffee on a Saturday morning. Anyone watching us in that moment could tell straight away that nothing else mattered but me. She drank me in so deeply I wished I could see myself as she did: the baby she'd cradled back in that dinky trailer on Spenard Road now stretched into a teen with a shaved head and piercings at nose and eyebrow. Her daughter still, but firmer. Fixed. You could never mistake me for an adult. With my turned-up nose and wide eyes, it would take another twenty years to look my age. Still, hardly any trace of childhood remained in my sixteen-year-old gaze.

"Hey, mama," I said, finally.

"Hey, daughter," she said.

The world exhaled, and we fell into each other, laughing.

I asked none of the thousand questions that had plagued me since I left. Could she see through Brian's charade yet? The way he'd promised to take care of her wounded heart and then slowly cut us off from everything: family and friends, our home, even music. Now she had become his full-time caretaker. Rent, groceries, and his medical bills all fell to her. Did she really believe, as he had, that I was so broken I could never be fixed? Or own any piece of regret for sending me away?

I didn't need to ask because right away, she said, "I love you forever." And I said, "Forever." After that, we were just two people chockfull of the knowing that growing up together brings. The rest would sort itself out.

We grabbed a bag each and turned to the exit, falling into step wordlessly. We knew where we were going. The airport might have burst into flames behind us for all we cared. We were lockstep, hand in hand, with home on our mind.

~

Back at the trailer on Fort Ord I found that my near-twin had been replaced by a teenager sporting elaborate black eye makeup, large hoop earrings, and brown lip liner. Tekla met us at the door in a baggy white T-shirt and khakis. She wore her strawberry blonde hair in a tight bun, accentuated by long bangs curled under. Salt-n-Peppa *shoop, shoop, ba-doop'd* at high volume in her back bedroom.

"Sissie!" she said, so tall now that she rested her chin on top of my head as we hugged. "Oh my gosh, your hair." She ran a hand through the inch of fuzz Alexis had just trimmed. "I can't tell if it's gross or cool?"

"Well, I got fired from my job at the hot dog stand for shaving it," I said. "So I guess . . . gross?"

"Holy shit. A job? Piercings?" She waved a hand around my face. "This is, like, *a lot*. Good thing you're not going to Seaside. You'd get your ass beat." She laughed, but there was no cruelty in it. "You would not blend in."

Her entire life had become about the blend. Seaside High School, at the height of the mid-90's gangsta rap scene, was an entirely other world from rural Alaska. Pants hung from hips, The Notorious B.I.G., Snoop Dogg, and Tupac blasted from car stereos in the parking lot. And bandana color mattered. Her voice had carried her into a close-knit circle of friends in chorus, where her kindness made up for being such an interloper. She had a place now.

Brian stood up from the couch, tobacco flakes dropping from a white shirt worn thin and yellowed with age. He approached as if interested in a hug, but I headed down the hall to my old room without a word. He'd had his say.

I fell right back into place in Monterey. Friends, theater, a job downtown at the Jamba Juice. An older boyfriend. Then I fell right back into place in Anchorage a few months later, when we all moved back north while Mom pursued a Master's in Education at Alaska Pacific University. I threw in the paltry three-thousand dollars I'd saved for a car to help with moving expenses instead. Except in Anchorage, I had more friends, a late-night job at the Roosevelt Café, an even older boyfriend, and zero desire to hear Brian's monotonous voice. They'd curtained off the dining room to create an extra bedroom in our tiny two-bedroom student housing unit, and his voice poured right through.

Mom dropped back into her studies with the kind of gratitude that a fresh student loan can bring after years of hustling to barely scrape by. "My classes are so amazing!" she'd gush in the evenings while Brian stirred up vegetables and brown rice in the tiny kitchen.

"Yeah, well, you've worked really hard for a lot of years," he'd say, rubbing her shoulder tenderly. "You deserve a break." She did, too. She deserved a break from the guy who wouldn't let her call up her old music friends. He refused to go out for a meal or a movie with her because it was a waste of money, yet he'd never had a paying job that I knew of. "I'm really happy for you, Fawn."

Then as she left the room, he'd turn to me with an expression he never wore when she was in sight. Something greater than disgust but less obvious than hate. "I suppose *you* want food, too?"

"Naw, I ate at work."

"Good. She doesn't have to suffer through dinner with you, then."

I saw no sign of suffering my company from my mother. We piled up on the couch with Tekla to read on weekend mornings, same as always. We took walks when the sun broke through the grey wall of late winter. Sometimes we still jumped in on those old-timey tunes when Mom tossed her books aside and pulled out her guitar. Mostly we spun in different circles, each of us preoccupied. I found things to keep me out of Brian's reach as school dragged my mother out of the house more and more.

"I know you're used to doing things on your own now," Mom said sometime toward spring. "But I don't love waiting up until ten to make sure you're home." There'd been not one instance of harshness between us since my return. She didn't feel the need to mother me anymore, and I hardly had time to notice the change.

Even this moment felt less parental and more like roommates catching up. We shared a blanket and a cup of hot, black coffee on the apartment's small balcony as slow Saturday morning traffic trundled by on Tudor Road.

"Oh . . . sorry. I had to work later than I planned last night," I said, taking the cup she offered. "I didn't mean to make you worry."

"You could call next time?" she said.

I had, but it was Why Are You Such a Piece of Garbage Brian who answered. I could never be sure my messages reached her. "Mmm, sure. You're *working*," he'd said. "I know you're out partying all the time. I'm not going to lie for you." Sometimes I did go to parties but, more than anything, I worked. Most of the time, I felt as though someone had stuffed me into the body of an anxious old lady. I rarely drank. And pot ratcheted up my anxiety. I worried about cops and disappointing my friend's parents equally. But I never felt I had to lie to Mom about parties.

"You really are gone a lot," she said, taking the cup back.

I shivered and tucked my arms under the shared blanket.

"I'm not staying away from *you*," I told her. "I'm staying away from Brian."

She sat for a moment, contemplating the steam rising from our cup.

"It's that bad?" she asked, finally.

I sighed. She loved him, and for that, I didn't want to hurt her. We watched traffic quietly. A city bus pulled up to the nearby stop, and a young woman climbed down, shook out a stroller, and buckled in a small crying child.

"This isn't working out, is it?" she said.

I wished she meant her and Brian, but I knew better.

I shook my head. "Not like this." We could have sailed an entire lifetime on the ocean of unshed tears between us.

A few months later, shortly before my seventeenth birthday, I moved into a basement apartment across town.

"You're awfully young," my landlord said. I'd met him through my job at the café. He worked on the ferries and was gone most of the time. "Are you sure you're up for this?"

"I don't know if I've ever really been young," I said, handing over my first month's rent. A kind of giddiness followed me down the stairs to my new room. I had a plan: I would start college instead of returning for my senior year of high school. I'd been at the mercy of the wind long enough. I wanted to know what it felt like to point myself in a direction of my own choosing and go there. And I didn't have to do it entirely alone. Mom was just a phone call or a thirty-minute walk away.

I unloaded my first box of clothes, recalling our drive to Fort Ord from the San Jose International Airport the year before. A thick fog had clung to Highway 1, surreal and heavy. Almost too much. Like we'd stumbled onto a horror movie set. Mom had leaned forcefully toward the windshield the entire drive, white-knuckling the steering wheel as if she could penetrate the gloom purely by will.

"This is almost as bad as blinding snow," she'd said.

Immense eucalyptus trees, Monterey pines, and coast live oaks had sporadically ghosted into focus through the vapor as we crawled south, leaping from the mist like monsters. Each time they sent lightning through my lungs until, finally, the familiar ringing in my ears that signaled a panic attack swept over me. I'd held my breath, wishing I could take the wheel. As much for some sense of control as to give my mother a break.

But I'd had a lifetime of road trips with my mother at the helm by then. We'd hiked through bitter snow and sideways rain. We'd slept countless nights pressed together in a nest of blankets while wind-chopped waters tilted at one ferry or another and woken to just as many bright mornings when the wind died down and the sun blazed in through our tent walls, or the boarding house windows, or the stained glass pane that had hung at the front of the bus.

Our whole life, we'd been moving toward each other and away and back.

Something had shifted into place during our time apart. I finally understood the one thing that had eluded my child's mind. If I could lean into the *not-knowing* with Mom, just let her drive, we'd always wind up where we needed to be in the end. Whether we shared a roof or not, we didn't have to be apart. It didn't have to be all or nothing.

I'd half expected to take a bite of the fog when I rolled my window down for fresh air on that drive, but it drifted in with a gentle eucalyptus breath and settled over us as a friend. The one-hour drive had stretched into three as we limped south toward Fort Ord. Mom held my hand the entire way.

Now, in my new room, I unfolded a hand-sewn quilt Mom had given me as a housewarming gift. Heavy and warm, it had bright green corduroy backing and large, wild patches of color over the front. It reminded me of the collage paintings she'd done back in Juneau. I pressed it to my nose, inhaling the eucalyptus and sandalwood soap smells that had worked into the fabric as she stitched each piece by hand. I laid it over my mattress on the floor and smiled. I was all the way home in a way I hadn't been in a long, long time.

As Long as You'll Have Me

~∽~

My mother's green quilt followed me out of my basement apartment at the end of summer when I moved in with my upstairs neighbor John and his five-year-old daughter, Ella. He was older than me, but the age difference troubled me not at all. I felt as though I'd been grown for a century, while boys my own age were still largely jobless and living at home.

John had a firmness I could lean into. He was an old-school pothead who'd come of age in the '80s. He'd lost his father young, and he carried a nostalgia for his youth that pawed at his ribs like a pack of caged pups. Best of all, he had Ella. Fierce Ella, with her bow lips and eyes the color of rubbed sage that shook a little when she looked at you sideways, nystagmus caused by an imbalance of tendon strength that has largely resolved with age. I'd spent a fair portion of the summer lounging on the couch in John's mother-in-law apartment, twisting up daisy chains with Ella. Generally being around. I ached at how easily she could launch into her father's lap, grab his face with her small hands and say, "I need a hug *right now*," and the ready way he always dropped what he was doing to comply. I pined for the closeness they shared.

I first babysat Ella the night after I lost my dishwashing job at the Roosevelt Café for leaving my post to deliver food and beer to customers.

"Bummer about your job," John said when he answered the door. Like everyone I knew, he was a regular at the Roosevelt. He knew I'd been fired practically the moment it happened. "Do you have any other job prospects?"

I shrugged. "For tonight, it's babysitting." I didn't have it in me to worry what would happen next, figuring I could afford my small basement room on any of the dozen or so minimum wage jobs in the paper. Still, I had bills to pay. The thought of all the working hours I'd waste looking for a new job left me vacant. And I'd have to wait on taking the GED. I'd needed that job badly.

After dinner, Ella and I moseyed out to the patchy yard and rolled in the grass, where she gleefully ground dandelions into my arms because I'd once told her they made me itch. A bald-faced lie. She'd already yellowed several shirts that I couldn't afford to replace any time soon.

At five, she had a child's preternatural ability to home in on precisely the thing you asked her to leave alone, as though to prove how not impressed she was with your authority. "Don't throw rocks at the neighbor's house," I'd say, and she'd look at me from the side of her face, eyes jiggling. Then she would turn and throw rocks *toward* the neighbor's house like, *Does it count if I don't hit the house?*

Oh boy, did I know that girl. She already had half the lines from the *Star Wars Trilogy* memorized. She favored Nirvana over children's music. A stack of yellowed *X-Men*, *Spider-Man*, and *Sandman* comics from her father's childhood sat perched on the dresser beside the bed they shared when she stayed with him. They were her preferred nighttime reading. She had one essential stuffed animal, Special, a black-and-white bunny John had given her. Somehow the pink ones hadn't suited her. Special went everywhere with Ella, hitching rides in her backpack to and from school on days she switched houses. Her parents were separated, having married when they found out they were pregnant, hoping for the best. Her mother, Danielle, now lived with her girlfriend across town.

Later that night, we wrestled on the couch, Ella practicing a piledriver maneuver on me while I protected my face. Then we watched *The Empire Strikes Back*. "You know it's bad when your own father cuts your hand off," Ella said in all seriousness. She lay in the crook of my arm, knobby knees wedged into my hip. I wondered how I could adore her so intensely that it sent flash fire through me. It felt like she'd always been mine or had always been meant for me. My mother had already been married once by my age, and suddenly I could see the appeal in something as fixed as a family of my own.

A week later, I babysat again. But this time, John came home with a serious look in his eyes. "Let me help you," he said. "Stay here with me." I knew I had other options, but none of them had an Ella. We passed five years that way.

Brian had a job offer in Hilo, Hawaii, and Mom stopped by with a box of books before she and Tekla joined him. She found me on the living room floor with Ella perched on my lap, smashing color onto the page. "Oh, this looks like fun," Mom said, joining us on the floor.

"We're making fireworks," Ella said, seriously. "They're going to explode off the page."

"That's the best kind of art," Mom said solemnly, catching my eye over Ella's head as if to say, *I see why this is good for you.* She would be in Hawaii for a year before returning to the Monterey Bay area again, where Tekla would finish out high school at Seaside High School. We'd never live in the same town again.

Of all the directions I might have spun at that young age, with all the unexplored freedoms of new adulthood opening up for me, this one drew me earthward. Down into the small, fierce center of Ella's child-sized universe. When Ella was with us, my focus shifted away from my part-time jobs to building forts and stacking rocks, and trying to outrun dandelion puffs on the wind.

One morning a couple years later, after we'd moved to a bigger house across town, Ella curled into my ribs like she always did. We'd pulled a blanket over us, and she was sounding out new words from a *Calvin and Hobbes* strip.

"T-E-M-P," she said, her eyes jiggling with focus. "T-A-T-I-O-N."

"The T-I makes a "sh" sound. Smoosh it together," I said, stroking the hair back from her forehead.

"Temp-taSHion?" she said. "What does that mean?"

"It means wanting to do something you know you shouldn't ..." I paused, a bright feeling humming through me, too fleeting to nail down.

"Why shouldn't Calvin play croquet?" Ella asked, drawing me from my thoughts.

I laughed.

"The joke here is that Hobbes thinks this is a gentleman's game because people with high manners like to play it instead of a rough sport like football. But does Calvin have good manners?"

Ella shook her head.

"Right. He wants to do something with that croquet mallet that he knows is a real bad idea."

"Like whack Hobbes with it," she smiled up at me over her glasses, waggling her eyebrows.

The feeling washed through me again, like the first whiff of a lilac bush blooming one block over before you realize spring has arrived.

"Let's see what he does," I said, pressing the book flat.

I saw my hand against the page, a miniature version of my mother's. The bright feeling coalesced, throwing me back to the first time I'd read this same strip. We'd had a month-long house-sitting gig at a friend's spacious home in Juneau. It had felt like a miracle to be in a house so full of elegant matching furniture. The kitchen was large and spotless. The kids' rooms were packed with books and toys I'd never seen before. I'd found several

Calvin and Hobbes books on the shelf and asked my mother about this very same joke. I knew what temptation was, but it had always been motivated more by a hunger for things I ached for that other kids took for granted. If a kid left their new roller skates on the sidewalk, why couldn't I take them?

"Does temptation make you a bad person?" I'd asked my mother.

She was sprawled on the deep couch with her feet in my lap, immersed in a book of her own. Her long hair lay coiled at her collarbone, and it shifted like a cat's tail when she moved. You could almost hear her purring.

She spread her hand flat across her book as if to keep the pages from wandering off. She looked up at me, brows drawing down thoughtfully. "I think temptation teaches you who you are," she'd said. "It's what you do with it that counts."

I looked at my fingers splayed out on the pages of *The Authentic Calvin and Hobbes* laying open across Ella's lap. The circle closed with an almost physical snap.

My hands are smaller and paler than my mother's. My summer stardust is a pink spray on ivory, where hers run olive and gold. Yet the whirling pattern of creases circling my thick knuckles and the slope of my broad palms are identical to hers. For a moment, it felt as though I had bent time, becoming child and mother at once. I recalled the sensation of curling into my mother's softness, her ribs at my elbow, and the scent of sandalwood in her hair, overlaid now by a new awareness of what she herself had felt with my small, bony frame tucked under her wing.

Ella lashed out with her feet, kicking the blanket from our laps and knocking the book to the floor.

"Whoah! What's that about?" I said.

"I'm hot," she said.

"Too much blanket?"

A slow flush spread up her cheeks, and she scratched at her arms. "Oh no!" She clutched at her face, leaving furious half-moons in her cheeks with her fingernails. She launched to her feet, flapping her hands like a flightless bird bent on escape. She wore one of her father's T-shirts, so long it fell to her knees. She gasped and reached inside the sleeve holes to scratch at her shoulders and chest. In a breath, her green eyes had gone glassy and begun leaping with stress. "No, no, no!"

She'd swung from calm to screaming quick as a bee sting.

Occasional bouts of sensory overwhelm weren't unusual for her. Too many layers in winter or the wrong fabric against her skin could unleash a full-body meltdown. But she was due to leave for her mother's house soon. Wild fits of anger and unquenchable tears had lately become regular events since Danielle had split up with her long-term girlfriend. The trick was catching them before Ella got enough wind under her to burn down an entire day.

She struggled with the shirt, fighting to pull it off.

"Are you hurt?"

"I'm hot. I'm hot. I'm hot!" she said, her entire face red now.

"Oh, you're overheating," I said, finally catching on. "Stand outside for a minute while I get you a glass of water."

"The sun is shining," she moaned. "That'll make it worse."

I coaxed her toward the door with a hand on her back. "Trust me," I said. "It's September. The air is plenty cold."

"No!" She shook me off, spinning away into the wall. "You're not my mom!" She slumped to the floor, heaving. She nearly always turned into me rather than away. For a moment, I found myself unable to think.

I opened the back door to let in air. Wild young birch trees flexed and bowed in the small yard beyond, yellow and orange leaves trembling in the breeze. In the kitchen, I grabbed ice from the freezer, a glass, dribbled cold water into the cup, and sat with her, careful not to add my own body heat to the fire. I held the glass up, but she pushed it away.

I looked at my hands for answers. They often seemed to know what to do before I did. How had they learned to care for a child so deeply? But I found only a glass of cold water, condensation weeping gently into my palm.

I knew the hurt she carried. I knew how it felt to drift on the winds of change stirred up by adults. I knew what it meant to *worry, worry, worry* that the people you loved might eventually find someone else to devote themselves to.

The breeze from the open door carried the scent of cold mornings and scattered leaves. I shivered, a line of gooseflesh running up my forearms.

"Still hot?" I twirled the glass so that the ice clinked.

Ella took in a shuddering breath and reached out a hand without raising her head. She took a sip. Another. A tear dropped quietly into the glass. She handed it back to me.

"No matter what happens, I'm yours forever," I told her. "I love you for your own self." It was the thing I'd always longed to believe in as a child.

She rocked sideways, drifting gently into my side and laying her head against my shoulder.

"You can be my kid without me having to be your mom. And that's the deal for as long as you'll have me."

"Which is forever," she said, drawing my arm around her. We sat for a while.

"I'm feeling a terrible temptation right now," I said, twirling the glass again.

Ella looked up at me sideways, only a little jiggle in her eyes now.

I raised the glass and waggled my eyebrows, giving her my most evil grin.

"I'm tempted to pour this entire freezing cold glass of water onto a certain wild-child and chase her around the house."

She threw a hand up, pretending to stop me, and let out the, *Are you serious? You're not serious!* laugh of a kid ready to tangle.

She held up a finger. "But I want to find out what happens when Calvin plays croquet first," she said.

~

John and I were engaged for three years, but he and Danielle had never gotten around to finalizing their divorce. Our wedding date came and went, and we never rescheduled. I'd taken a full-time position at the medical library on campus at the University of Alaska, Anchorage, which allowed me to work around my classes. I loved the smell of dusty books and ancient carpeting, but the perpetual silence rattled me. I listened to books on tape to break up the monotony of shelving medical journals.

I made dinner after work, packed lunches, and did homework with Ella on her nights with us. John's summer work left him with a lot of free time in the winter, which he spent playing early versions of online role-playing games on the computer. We only had one computer, so I experimented with new recipes, sewed curtains, and grew a garden of books. Our life turned me further inward than I thought possible. I hadn't seen the inside of a tent or felt the press of strangers at a crowded folk festival in years. I missed people.

John and I weren't soul mates. We weren't even particularly much alike. We were companions. Five years in, I realized I'd gone missing from myself. What use were a stack of books taller than me without a story of my own?

I stayed for Ella. Longer than I would have otherwise. Grandma Gorgeous Darling had married at fifteen to escape the rigid confines of her grandmother's farm. Mom had already divorced her abusive first husband by the time she turned nineteen. I could see what had brought me to my relationship with John. I could also see it, if only in outline, for the cycle it was.

"You promised you'd never leave," Ella said when I picked her up from school after I'd moved out. Tears ran freely down the neck of her hoodie as she stared out the window. "But I know you needed to go." I felt her sorrow as keenly as if she'd opened her ribs and placed my hands on her heart.

~

I had never expected Thom would move on with his life so completely. He'd remarried, had two more boys, and built a world so far
from mine he might as well have been terraforming some forbidden
moon in a galaxy far, far, away. And he'd said he'd be mine forever.

I had something else in mind when I made that promise to Ella.

"The deal stands," I said, turning onto Fireweed Lane. "For as
long as you'll have me."

"Which is forever," she said, reaching blindly for my hand.

The heater in my grey Chevy Cavalier station wagon battled a
late-winter cold front as we wound toward my new place near the
University.

"I don't even remember my life before you," she sighed. She had
turned ten a few months earlier. She kept her dark hair long and
loose, favored sweatshirts paired with black jeans, and she stood
taller than me already. We'd been trading clothes for years by then.

"I know," I said, squeezing her hand. "We're working it out so
that you can stay with me every week. As long as you want to."

"Which is forever," she said again, rolling her eyes and letting a
corner of her mouth turn up. Her eyes were wet with heartache but
jiggled not at all.

She had three homes to choose from after that.

I might have spun any direction from there. I knew I had other
options. I could have said, *You still have two good parents, kid. I need
to live my own life now.* I could have taken the easy route and slipped
quietly away like Thom had.

I had other options. But none of the good ones had an Ella in it.
So when I left, I stayed.

Figure in Red

~·~·~

Eight years earlier, Tekla and I had stood outside our older brother's apartment. We had just left C.A. in Juneau and moved to Anchorage. We were tagging along with Mom on a weed hunting mission.

"Do you think he'll recognize us?" Tekla whispered as she knocked. I doubted it. We'd spent a little time with Zach years before when we'd driven down from Fairbanks for the Alaska State Fair. After the fair, we'd passed a week bumbling through Dude's neighborhood on a getting-to-know-you mission, as shy and prone to bolting for hidey-holes as the wild cats that prowled his garden. We'd marveled at Zach and Cimberlee, siblings so much older than us that they'd felt more like a long-lost aunt and uncle. We'd shared a few awkward hugs with Dude and played with the kids across the street. Other than that, I couldn't remember much of that strange dream of a visit. I couldn't imagine we'd left much of an impression on Zach in such a short time. Besides, Tekla and I had each grown a foot taller since then.

In his mid-twenties, Zach wore black-rimmed glasses and let his hair fall to his shoulder blades in natural ringlets the color of an oak tree in shadow. He held a Marlboro Red in one hand and a cheap beer in the other when he opened his door. Mom hid behind the door frame so we could surprise him.

"Oh, cute," Zach said when he found us at his threshold. "Little girls." He took a swig of beer. "What are you selling?" His voice tended toward the sweet-soft whisper of a peaceful pothead.

"Do you know who we are?" Tekla asked, dancing on the balls of her feet. Her hair hung long and straight over a droopy alpaca sweater from Mom's booth at the Haines music festival.

Zach smiled a sweet *nobody's-home* stoner smile. "No," he said, a touch of Minnesota in his "O." I suppose he picked up the accent honestly since I later learned Dude had grown up in Minnesota. Behind him, I could see a bong on the coffee table. Smoke drifted lazily on a current made by the open door.

A wrinkle creased Zach's brow, and he pushed his glasses up with a pointer finger. "Actually . . . you kind of look like my dad." He squinted, looking us over more carefully. "Holy cow." You could almost see the zenned-out generator of his mind dragging sluggish cogs into action. "Are you my sisters?"

Tekla squealed and gave him a friendly half-hug. I resisted the urge to roll my eyes. Just what we needed. More stoners in our lives.

"Dude, you won't believe this," Zach said over his shoulder. "Your daughters are here."

I was so stunned I might have failed to notice if the walls around me turned to flowers. How had I not seen this coming?

Zach swung his door wide to reveal a mountain of a man lounging on one side of a threadbare plaid couch.

Dude wore a flannel shirt buttoned over a white tee and tucked into camouflaged cargo pants. Wet red curls sprang from beneath a tattered ball cap, and sweat dripped from his brow, which I would soon learn always happened in temperatures above fifty degrees. Dude looked like Paul Bunyan if Paul Bunyan had been a pothead. He blew a puff of smoke over his shoulder, waggled scruffy eyebrows at us, spread his arms, and dropped his jaw in a great big Howdy-Doody smile.

"Wow," he said, drawing us in for a hug. "*Wow.*" He planted a smokey, wet kiss on my cheek and patted my backside affectionately while I stood there, confusion pinning me to the floor. I didn't know whether that was normal fatherly behavior or if I had a right to object. *How weird,* I thought. *That's my estranged father's hand caressing my butt. What the hell happens now?*

If I were inclined toward seeing a divine hand at work, I might have questions about how and why my father reappeared in my life just then. But my mind doesn't run toward mystery very easily. Particularly because the very thing that separated us had brought us full circle: Mom had needed weed.

I was done looking for a dad by the time Dude reappeared in my life. You weren't going to find me hunched over a fishing pole talking about the birds and the bees with this virtual stranger. I needed more than a genetic link to bridge the years of dead air between us. I never did figure out what the missing element was. The road back to each other only ever seemed to run in circles.

I couldn't make sense of my father: his lifestyle, his intellect, his history. He drank curdled milk. He ate food that had gone green and squishy with age. He'd sung opera and studied the bible in preparation for seminary school, but had come to Alaska on a fishing trip one summer during the fight for statehood and never left.

One year I met a friend of Dude's at the Talkeetna Folk Festival who gave me a rusty button that read *Carlson, of course!* in blue ink over a tarnished white background. I learned that Dude had run for Congress three times: 1982, 1984, and 1986. During his first campaign Dude ran against Don Young, garnering substantial support for an unknown entrant with 52,000 votes. Yet it seemed the more I learned about him, the more of a mystery he became.

During the ten months I'd lived with Zach, my father and I had developed a rhythm. I visited him randomly; he called every few months. I didn't particularly like going to Dude's house because I couldn't shake the paranoia of an undercover cop car parked some-where nearby, watching me.

I always found myself rehearsing what I'd say if a cop approached me. *He's my father. I don't live here. I barely even know the guy. I swear I'm not buying pot.*

When friendly clients stopped by during my visits, he'd draw me close in a breath-stealing hug and beam. "Have you met my daughter?"They'd take in his arm around my shoulders, me squirm-ing against him with a half-smile, regretful that I'd let myself get close enough for him to catch me by surprise. You could see that the revelation of a long-lost daughter left them with questions. Me too, given that he'd frequently just finished saying something like, "You're just another cog in the wheel, kid. Too bad. What a waste," before his customer had shown up.

We carried that routine forward when I moved into my first apartment three years later. I could walk to his place in under five minutes, but I rarely did. I asked if he'd cosign for student loans when I started college at eighteen. I couldn't apply for them on my own until I turned twenty-four unless I became formally emanci-pated, which felt like a lot of hassle. He declined. "What a stupid idea," he'd said.

"College?"

"Yeah. And why would I agree to pay off your loans if you default? Which you're going to do. I don't even know how you're paying rent." He said this despite the three part-time jobs he knew I worked.

I hadn't expected anything else. Mom, now back in California with Tekla and Brian, couldn't help either. "I can't take on any more student debt," she'd said apologetically. "I can barely handle what I already owe." I took the out-of-pocket route instead, saving through the summers and taking only as many classes as I could afford. It took nearly ten years to graduate.

When I did visit Dude I had to wander around the yard and shout up at the windows to get his attention. He couldn't hear a fist pounding on the front door due to the mounds of detritus in there absorbing soundwaves like so much Jell-O.

The city had been trying to raze that two-story eyesore for years. The interior was worse than the trailer we'd lived in when I was born. Every single room was filled with junk from floor to ceiling, at least half of it literally trash. A foot-wide path snaked through the maze, which Dude occasionally, and meticulously, vacuumed. Wild cats bore kittens in the holes in his walls.

Behind the house, he maintained a large vegetable patch. Broccoli, cauliflower, tomatoes, kale, catnip, carrots, and sundry other leafy things grew fat and juicy beneath a massive lilac tree in the summer. The garden's carefully maintained rows stood in sharp contrast to the rusted-out refrigerators and random car parts stacked around it.

He spent most of his time in that yard, sweating over a rake or tapping golf balls into empty soup cans. Friends visited all day, every day. Often staying late into the night. They sat on dusty chairs to drink beer, smoke pot, and toss horseshoes. I can't guess where they sat during the winter.

On one visit, I had pounded my hand to bruises and started to turn away when the door finally cracked open. "Oh! It's you," Dude said. His eyes shone bluer than blue, as though lit from within. He wore his standard uniform: unbuttoned flannel over a T-shirt and army fatigues.

"Just starting the first fire of the year," he said, ceremoniously waving a wad of newspaper. He hugged me with his free arm, crooking my head into his armpit. Garlic and onion smells rose stale and manly from his clothes.

The burn-door of his massive wood stove stood open as we stepped inside. Tendrils of flame reached out, hungry for air. Sparks popped. I rushed to close up the stove, but he stopped me with a wave, already ranting about a guy clear-cutting trees somewhere.

"People are disgusting," he raved. "They don't care what they waste. All they want is money. What good is money when all your damn trees and animals are gone?" His chest heaved, causing his stomach—firm and round as an oaken keg—to rise and fall. He hit a joint and went quiet, pressing a can of Budweiser between his knees.

My father wept for the world. His tangents, I'd learned, ran a thin line between paranoid conspiracy theories and a righteous desire to protect the planet from mankind. I understood his frustration, but the fury that came with it always put a little tremble in my gut. I could never be sure he wasn't angry at me when I caught him in mid-tirade like that.

He ushered me into a rusty lawn chair tucked into a tiny clearing beside the fire. It gave me a precarious feeling. Somewhere against the wall, there was a couch, I knew. Unmarked bags and boxes towered ceiling-high around us. Here a bag of brightly colored beads and porcupine quills. There, a pile of ivory, unidentified fur pelts, and woodcarvings.

Every room was the same, except one in the back corner that sizzled with grow lights and greenery. Decapitated milk jugs lined the stairs to the second floor, ready to serve as chamber pots. Newspapers dating to the late sixties stood sentinel beside the bed I was born on twenty-something years earlier, in a trailer a few blocks away. The bed my father still slept in.

"Oh!" he boomed, oblivious to the way I jumped in my seat. "I gotta show you something." He disappeared upstairs, returning with a large square print loosely wrapped in tissue that he peeled off to reveal a portrait.

"Your mom did this the year you were born."

He handed it to me, and I sucked in air. It was a full-length nude portrait of my father, drawn in red charcoal on thick white paper, the bold lines suggesting this strong man had known how to be a lover. He sat partially turned away, and you could see that every stroke was a story. The curve of his back was a promise; the muscles of his arms and legs an elegy. The figure glowed with an attention to detail that my mother only invests when she is enamored by her subject and wants to sit with the page. This piece had been a declaration.

If I had the ability to travel in time, I might choose that moment. My father posing for my mother, him laughing, her saying, "*Don't move, don't move!*" The dreams they shared.

I wanted to steal it. To hang it on the wall above my bed and study it. I wanted to know the man he'd been when my mother first knew him before all the years of hard drinking and paranoia had put holes in him. It seemed this likeness could tell me things. Important things. I could ask my young father: Would you have made me if you'd known I'd grow up without you? Did you want me then, the way I wish I could want you now?

On that visit, I stayed until the secondhand high set my heart jackrabbiting against my ribcage. Dude didn't seem to notice my distress. He leapt from topic to topic, pausing only to hit a joint or stir the fire anxiously.

The room began to feel like a trash compactor inching shut. I found myself vaguely amused and horrified by the thought of a person crushed to death by all that *stuff*. An avalanche could happen any moment. You wouldn't find a body in there for weeks.

Dude walked me six feet to the door, and I hugged him because isn't that what daughters do? His eyes were red, his breath beery. As he hugged me, one hand slipped to my butt, and his kiss wandered from my cheek to my ear. I cringed as he stuck his tongue in there. The muscles at the back of my neck seized, gluing my tongue to the roof of my mouth. Had I the power of speech in that moment, what would I have said? He was not Ray, and I knew it. My discomfort ranged more toward disgust than offense.

I wondered whether my father had ever understood what his absence had wrought in my life. What if he'd given up the dealer gig and gone straight? Had let Mom empty the trailer and fill it with decent furniture and happy children? Instead, we had come to this: a drunk old man groping the daughter who's student loans he wouldn't cosign.

I clamped one hand to my ear and pawed at the tattered blanket that hung over the warped front door for extra insulation. I found the doorknob and escaped into a furious wind, white-knuckled and shaking.

In retrospect, I should have stopped right there at the front door and laid some ground rules for our future: Pretend you like me if you have to. Yell at someone else. And my ass is off-limits. Always.

But I said nothing because I feared his anger.

I never felt good about it when the months without contact stacked up. Sometimes I laid awake, worrying at this thing between us, promising myself I'd call soon. Somehow, I never did. When I left for Virginia with my boyfriend a few years after I finished college, it never occurred to me to call my father and say goodbye. I'd told him I would be leaving several months earlier. It had seemed sufficient.

I didn't call when I heard his house caught fire either. I meant to, but I was chasing a romantic dream across the country. A fire. And Dude's house so full of junk they could only let it burn. I wondered if that portrait, the one in red charcoal, survived. I could see it so clearly, the bold strokes of his beard and his broad back crisping. Fire nibbling the edges until, with one hot bite, there was nothing left but ash. The man who made me, the man I could never know. Gone forever.

Heart Conditions

~⌐~

I didn't get a lot of personal calls at the medical library and never from Zach, so it came as a surprise when he called me out of the blue one morning.

"Dad's in the hospital," he said, his voice rough as a hangover. "I can't get there until tonight. I don't want him to die alone."

Dude had been watching the Vikings on the big screen at Pancho's Villa, a restaurant situated one block over from his house. He'd started the game with a homemade pot brownie, which he followed up quickly with 44 ounces of draft beer. By halftime, the Vikings were down, and so was Dude. He toppled to the floor and laid still as death until the paramedics arrived, jumpstarted his heart, and then carted him off to Alaska Regional Hospital.

I arrived minutes behind the ambulance and asked for Dude. The woman behind the counter kindly informed me that they had a lot of "dudes" in the I.C.U. at the moment, and could I be more specific? I struggled to recall his given name. I'd never used it. He'd always been a nickname kind of guy to me.

I found him lying beneath a thin blanket in his room, rivers of sweat dripping from his forehead. As ever, his thin red-gray curls clung damp and springy at his temples. At sixty-three, he was still a man of football-playing proportions. The hospital gown strained against his broad chest, and his feet hung from the bed as though they'd accidentally given him a child's cot. His eyes were all iris: a hard, blue pinball that darted ceaselessly from the light ballast to a beeping heart monitor, to the door, to me, to the bathroom.

Dude managed to still his gaze enough to look at me and raise one gnarled paw to his mouth. "I ate a *huuuge* pot brownie," he said in a big whisper. "And a giant beer. There's nothing wrong with me."

I nodded agreeably, wishing I could blame the brownie too. But the doctors had diagnosed A-fib before they'd even finished unloading the crash cart at Pancho's. Atrial fibrillation is a condition that causes the upper portion of the heart to beat rapidly—faster and more frequently than the lower chambers. The fluttering sensation leads to dizziness, shortness of breath, and utter terror.

Something else troubled my father's heart, though. Something truly broken that caused his blood pressure to drop until he'd crashed, repeatedly, on the ride to the hospital.

I considered leaning over to kiss him on the cheek, but his body odor, a rich, oniony musk, rubbed up against the antiseptic hospital smells of Lysol, bleach, and plastic machinery. I took his hand instead.

"They want me to get a pacemaker," Dude said. His eyebrows rose up conspiratorially before collapsing, folding together in consternation. Again, he cupped his mouth with one big hand. "They want to make me a robot," he whispered. I couldn't help wondering how, at twenty-three years old, I'd become responsible for this grown-ass man-child.

"This is not a conspiracy," I whispered, fighting back an involuntary eye roll. "These people want to save your life."

His expression took on the round-eyed sulk of a dog smacked on the nose by a beloved friend. Could he trust me? Had I been compromised? Had I become one of them, the pill pushers from Big Pharma?

I wished for rescue. For Zach or Cim to come sit with our father instead of me.

A nurse entered, handing Dude a small paper cup and several pills. A young doctor trailed in behind her, flipping charts on his clipboard.

"Alright," he said without looking up. "We need to take some pictures of your heart." He slapped a blank monitor sitting near the head of the bed. Dude flinched. "It's a simple procedure. We're going to perform a transesophageal echocardiogram."

"A what?"

The doctor smiled. "We'll send a little camera down your throat and take a video of your heart. Don't worry," he chuckled, pointing at the pills in Dude's hand. "One of those will knock you out, and the other will make you forget. You won't remember a thing."

Dude murmured, nodding his head in false agreement, grasping his bedsheet in one hand. A good little boy. He didn't want to know what was going on. He wanted only to say *yes* the right number of times to spring himself from the hospital. His eyes began jumping around the room again. He had the look of a man planning his escape even as he swallowed the pills.

He waited until morning and walked out of the hospital when the doctors weren't looking. He called me at work to explain.

"Those doctors don't know anything," he said. "They're not going make me a robot."

Anger scalded the air in my lungs. "Do you have a death wish?" I seethed. Co-workers turned to stare, eyebrows raised, mouths parted in shock. Libraries aren't the place for noisy displays. I hunched guiltily behind my monitor to hiss.

"You're a menace with a heart like that! What if you're *driving* the next time your heart stops?" Which is exactly what did happen a few days later. Luckily, he swerved into a ditch rather than oncoming traffic.

That time the doctors forcibly installed a pacemaker. I didn't want to sit with him again. I didn't want to be the caretaker child. Cim and Zach grew up with Dude. They fished and smoked weed and drank together out in the backyard among the rusted-out cars and cast-off refrigerators. They shared the same friends. They'd tried to include me over the years, but I still felt like a working dog trying to fit in with a passel of cats in a field of catnip.

I found Dude in the hospital shortly after the pacemaker's installation, wildly transformed from the hardy man he'd been a few days earlier. He lay still, strong arms limp at his sides. He seemed smaller somehow. As though he'd been folded in two and flattened with an iron. I didn't need a medical degree to see how the strain on his body and the drugs coursing through his blood were taking a toll.

When his eyes rolled open briefly, his pupils were black holes that swallowed me. He'd been resuscitated three times in two days. I wondered what he'd seen on the other side of death.

The thought that he might die and we would never be more than we were right then invited hot tears to my cheeks, surprising me. I squeezed his cold left hand. The heart monitor beeped erratically: sometimes fast, sometimes slow. My own pulse echoed the beeps. Anticipating.

I did not want to be standing there when it stopped for good.

He woke slowly, eyelids jumping a few times before parting with great effort, like the Red Sea rolling back. "You are so beautiful," he said throatily. "You look like your mother."

His words fell on me like a down comforter in January.

He lay there, pale beneath a sheen of sweat. I felt tenderness for him. A new feeling. I liked it. For the first time since I'd met him, it seemed maybe I could love him as a daughter does.

"Will you marry me?" he asked, eyes drooping shut again.

"What?" I snatched my hand away.

"I know," he said, seeming to recognize me for the first time. "That was over the line." I pressed my legs into the wall behind me to give the anger somewhere to go. I wanted to walk out, but the sight of his eyes drifting shut again and the muscles at his neck going limp nailed me to the wall. I'd been in Anchorage for most of a decade by then, and still, he felt like a stranger. This old man. My father. Alone in a foreign land populated by machines and short-tempered nurses. What I would give for him to love me. What I would give to love him back.

Years later, my mother would tell me how my father had routinely proposed to people when he felt overwhelmed with affection. "He'd say to the cat: 'I love you, cat! You're so amazing! Marry me!' It was just his way." I didn't know that part of his story, though. And there's no guidebook for finding your way back from a surprise marriage proposal from your estranged father.

The heart monitor beeped on in the silence between us.

Six years later, we all gathered in Anchorage to meet Camden's newborn daughter. I picked Tekla up at the airport, and we swung through the grocery store to stock up on supplies for the visit. There he was, as if summoned by the very act of avoidance: our father. I spied him in the dairy aisle, limping slightly and holding a stiff left arm awkwardly at his side.

"I'm not ready to talk to him yet," Tekla whispered, tugging me toward the registers. Her cheeks went pink, and her gaze roved around the store as though afraid we might get caught dodging our own father. She hadn't spoken to him in nearly a decade. When she'd married her first husband several years earlier, it hadn't occurred to her to invite him. "Was I supposed to?" she'd asked me after the ceremony. How could I let her spend the rest of her life worrying, as I did, that she'd failed to connect with him?

I grasped her hand and led her down the dairy aisle, past the sour cream and buttermilk, calling to Dude as we reached the eggs. His blue eyes went wide, and he grabbed Tekla in his good right arm. He hugged her as though an electric current ran through his body, and she was the only thing that could ground him.

"Dudesy," she said, smiling into his flannel shirt. Later she told me she really thought *Dad* but had never said it before and couldn't say it then. Between one breath and the next, she went limp. She pressed her face into his chest and sailed into safe harbor between his ribs. A place I never knew existed.

Tekla and Dude stood silently at the border between cheese and eggs, tears in their eyes. I envied my sister her easy heart. For her, there had only ever been his absence, and now this. She was ready, and he was ready. They could simply love one another. I could only watch.

My heart mewled like an orphaned kitten. But I had been hurt by him.

I'd already been in town for a month by then, visiting friends. A few days earlier, I'd bumped into Zach and learned of Dude's strokes. I'd meant to reach out sooner but had delayed for the chore of it. A few hours later, Dude had called, screaming into the phone in a post-stroke rage. "I'm your *dad*. You should have called. You owe me that."

"You might be my father," I'd said, my hand shaking as I gripped the phone to my ear, "but you haven't earned the right to demand anything from me."

The pure honesty of it had felt like the beginning of something.

At the end of our visit that summer, we gathered in Talkeetna on the property Dude had given us years before to make good on a lifetime of outstanding child support. The drive up had been hot. Dude, Zach, Tekla, Mom, and I were all crammed in Dude's ancient Suburban, a case of PBR in the backseat between my knees.

The property is a small rectangle of densely wooded land, just over five acres. We gathered close in a sunny patch beneath spruce and birch trees, waving arms in unison to ward off mosquitoes. We'd never had a family outing like this before.

Sweat dripped from Dude's nose as he crouched to sit on a fallen log. Sweat soaked his shirt, leaving dry creases at his ribcage and the two inches around his belt line. We'd hiked around the property from edge to edge, fantasizing about where to build a dock on the lake, where the communal gathering lodge with its big kitchen and living room would go. We staked out imaginary plots for individual cabanas. Far enough apart for privacy, but near enough to feel close and connected.

"He does love you," Mom had told me the day before. We were in Aunty Jolette's backyard, drinking wine around the fire pit and planning the drive to Talkeetna. "I don't think he understands why you don't know it."

I'd thought of all those silent years stretched out between birth and when I moved to Anchorage at fourteen. Sure, Mom had left him. But how hard could it be to dial eleven digits and fill the gap? I recalled his tirades against my hopes for college. The way he could scream at me like I was a personal representative of the oil industry ravaging our natural resources. Could it be that I had simply never brought myself to heel and learned to walk the landscape of his mind? But a familiar heat had burned through me at the thought. Why should the repair work fall to me?

"Maybe," I'd said.

With all of us together on the property, it didn't seem impossible that we could build a family retreat there among the pines. Maybe my future children would get to know their grandfather in ways I never could.

He died six weeks later.

The next year, Tekla and I stalked the property vigilantly, searching for the exact log we'd sat on with Dude the year before. We wanted some of our father's ashes to return to the family land. We waded through the undergrowth in search of landmarks, but late summer made fools of us. The blueberries and fiddlehead ferns were so lush and green you almost couldn't believe anyone had ever walked there before. We spread out, trailing fine gray ash behind us like flower girls with rose petals. We traced the perimeter in opposite directions, welcoming our father home.

A raven followed me for a time, making short, fluttery hops between the trees to call down to me. *Crrrrroooo-kuk*, it said. *Crrrrroooo-kuk. No.*

"I know," I told the bird. "I'm sad, too." The bird ruffled its feathers and hopped sideways. Somehow, I'd done it all wrong with Dude. I'd thought there would be more time.

"Do you ever imagine how different things would be if we'd grown up with Dude?" Tekla asked when we circled back around to each other. Tear tracks lined her face, but her eyes were dry. She took a sip from the ceremonial can of Rainier we'd brought in his honor.

I nodded, accepting the can from her. "It would've been a whole other level of hard."

I'd only begun to understand that what he'd given me with his absence had been my mother. The years we'd spent traveling and chasing music, ferrying between festivals with Mom, had been a gift. We wouldn't have had Camden to love and miss so fiercely if we'd stayed with Dude. I might not have learned to make family where I could, to sleep on top of a guitar case when rain flooded the tent, or that I could make a home anywhere. Still, I mourned the loss of what we might have been, given time.

A small birch sapling stood alone on a little rise nearby. It was barely wide around as my wrist and verging on first blush. Finger-wide curls of ochre bark peeled away, thin to the point of translucence, blurring the line where the tree ended and sky began. Left to its own devices, that tree would live as long as us. Longer maybe. It might grow to seventy or eighty feet, casting its cool shade onto our children and their children, its many leaves clapping with the wind for generations.

The raven circled back and cocked its head at us from a perch in the canopy.

At the base of the young tree, I laid a thin rope of ash, poured beer into the moss at my feet, and raised the can high. "We were close to something, Dude," I said.

Crrrrroooo-KuK, the raven said. *Yes.*

"Crrrrroooo-KuK," I said to the bird, raising the can higher in acknowledgment.

"Oh my gosh," Tekla laughed. "You still do that?"

I laughed too. "Only when it feels right," I said. She laid her head on my shoulder.

A breeze riffled the lake's surface, tossing golden light from blue, green waters. I took my sister's hand, and we made our way back to the car, letting the wind carry our tears to their next life.

Bones

~~~

I am my mother's daughter in the end. It's as much a choice as anything else.

"I feel like you think I'm a failure as a mother," Mom said a few years ago. It seemed to come out of nowhere at the time, but I know now the hurt had been boiling up since I started writing.

We were ferrying from Ketchikan to Juneau, camped out on the solarium deck like the old days, visiting friends and family on our way to Anchorage. We'd planned the trip as a present to ourselves for making it so far: me out of grad school and her into a teaching career she loved in California.

We'd just stepped onto the solarium deck when Mom burst out: "I didn't mean to be the bad guy in your story." The steel door slammed behind us emphatically. "I didn't mean to do it all so wrong." I glanced at the other campers on deck, but they were either deep sleepers or very good actors. They seemed oblivious to the way the air between us had suddenly grown as hot and dry as a blast zone. "I did the best I could, you know," she said finally.

I owned the heart of a deer.

"Sometimes I feel like you could've done better for us," I said, blinking back panic at the suddenness of her anger. I imagined how differently our lives might have gone had she picked a place and stayed there or taken a job for the steady paycheck instead of the artistic opportunities. What would it have been like to have a friendship that lasted longer than a year? To grow up knowing my father?

We shared a long silence along the rails, wind in our eyelashes, sea spray salting our cheeks. We stood without moving, nosing at the danger in the air until tears eventually sent us to our separate tents.

Hours later, Mom unzipped my tent and leaned in. "I'm sorry," she said, reaching in to stroke my hair.

I rolled to a sit, half out of my sleeping bag, and knuckled my eyes. "I'm sorry too," I said. "Maybe you *could* have done things differently." I imagined her stuck in Dude's crowded home or hunched in a cubicle somewhere, wondering *what if?*

"But maybe you wouldn't have survived it."

My mother without art, without music, the phantoms of her childhood chasing her all over one small town? Inconceivable.

"We survived, though," I said. "All of us. It was hard, but we survived it."

I laid my head on her lap, and she resumed stroking my forehead. "That's my favorite feeling ever," I said.

She nodded down at me, the light from the overhead heat lamps casting an orange blush over the grey in her short hair. Her gaze fell softly on me as she brushed my bangs back, a half-smile at her lips.

"I know," she said.

"All I've ever wanted my entire life was to be your girl, no matter what," I said. "And we never let go, even when we had the chance. Wouldn't that have been the failure?"

What if ours hadn't turned out to be a love story, replete with hardship and heartbreak and a rickety, redemptive ending? We might as easily have fallen on our stubborn swords and spent our lives buried to the hilt in recrimination and blame. Instead, whenever a storm blew us off course, we'd simply steered into the wind until the horizon offered us clear passage again.

~

Music brings us back to each other more than anything else. Last year we decided we needed an excuse to visit Camden and Sarah in Juneau, so Tekla booked us a gig and a radio spot to promote her new album.

We practiced in Camden's small living room, Mom, Tekla, and her husband, Jeff, himself a renowned musician, and me. Tekla's voice remained high and firm and practiced, while my own had grown unreliable from years of disuse.

"You play," Camden told us. "We'll keep the kids busy." Sarah dragged our daughters into the kitchen to bake cookies. Camden waved to his teenage son, Ralleigh, holding up my six-month-old and an infant carrier. "Let me show you how to carry a baby, kid."

"If you can get him to sleep in that thing, I'll pay you good money," I promised my nephew. He flashed me a dimpled half-smile.

We jammed every night, playing through Mom's old-timey tunes and teaching each other our own compositions.

"The only thing I love more than playing songs you girls have written is playing them *with* you," Mom said. And the look in her eyes said, *I've never made anything in all my life as beautiful as you.* Her hair hung long and silver over her shoulder, but the smile in her wide eyes still sparked with youthful exuberance. C.A. rubbed her back, quietly beaming at us from his seat next to her on the couch.

Until recently, I'd only seen C.A. a handful of times since we left Juneau. Mostly during layovers. On one visit, we'd met for lunch, and after the waiter left with our order, he'd said, "I have a bunch of your old journals when you're ready for them."

"You kept those?"

"Of course," he'd chuckled. "You've always been my daughter." Then his face had softened as his eyes traveled through time. "Your mom will always be my wife." It had surprised me to learn the depth of his feelings for us, given our years of bickering. Though I still blamed my stubborn heart for most of the trouble between us.

"Naw, you weren't a bad kid," C. A. said. "I just didn't know what I was doing."

In the twenty-four years since we'd left C.A., he'd torn down our decrepit old house out on North Douglas, built a new one, quit drinking for a long stretch, retired from a job he loved at the Alaska Department of Transportation, and started drinking again, but with a moderation he hadn't had before. Then, when opportunity struck a couple of years ago, he wooed Mom back to Juneau after a lot of unsubtle nudges from Tekla and me. I've never seen anything to rival it in all my life. Their companionship now owns every kind of peace I've ever wished for my mother.

Thom stopped in while we practiced the night before our show and all of the grandkids climbed him like a tree trunk. "Hold on, hold on," he said, laying a sideways grin on each of them. "I'm not as spry as I used to be." He got down on the floor and sprawled out so that Camden's older kids could help my younger ones crawl all over him. During a break between songs, I looked down to find him holding my son in the air, tears standing in his eyes.

"Imagine what we could do if we all lived in one place for a while," Tekla said wistfully. Mom strummed her baritone ukulele and winked at me. Each of our growing-up-together years showed in that one small gesture. In all our time apart, through marriages and kids and across state lines, there'd never been a moment we weren't inextricably bound, my mother and brother and sister and me. But I knew now that between the four of us, the *peapod*, we simply had too much get up and wander for any one place to hold us long. Home remained a place we could only sing our way into.

I now own a house with my husband that rings with music and the laughter of our children, yet the homeless dream persists. I still search for hours, sometimes an entire night, for a place to call my own, but I find myself walking into that dream now with something like a sigh of recognition. I know the shape of that in-between place better than some of the homes I've actually occupied. Even the fear that comes with it is an old friend.

I wake from this dream with sadness, but also new risen. Because the loneliness of it is tempered by a fire that burns away the fog. My waking mind sees what my weary sleeping self cannot: though I have never found a home in this dream, I have never quit trying.

Maybe Mom and I don't hold the high notes the way we used to, but with Tekla there to lead us, we find them eventually. We don't care how long it's been, how dusty our voices are, how far apart we've been. We sing like we know what we are doing.

Acknowledgements

~~~

I handed my mother the first draft of this book several years ago, saying, "I never have to publish this." She read it through the night, and I woke up intermittently to the sound of her laughing and crying in the room next door. In the morning she hugged me. "This is your story," she said. "It's beautiful. It's hard. It's true. You don't need my permission to tell it. But you have it, if you want it." I may never be able to thank my mother adequately for the freedom she has given me to tell the story of our growing-up-together years.

I owe a lifetime of thanks to the rest of my family. To Tekla and Camden—best friends, siblings, minions—for living this adventure with me and for always giving me the best berries. To Zach and Cim, siblings I share too few memories with. To Aunty Jolette for her faith, and Grandma Gorgeous Darling for her love. To Ella, daughter of my heart, for the magic she's brought to my life. To my dads: C.A. for holding my notebooks all these years, and Thom, for holding my bike steady when I needed it. And to my father, Dude, into whose absence I first began to write.

To my made families: this would be a small life without you in it. I am so grateful for the sister who chose me, Alexis Roberts-Keiner, and her parents, Malcom and Cindy Roberts, who gave me new eyes when I needed them and still call me daughter to this day. Adán Hernandez has been the master of safe spaces and mixed tapes since before I knew I needed them. Lily Hope's love and friendship transports me back to childhood like no one else. Liz Boeheim, Becky Margolis, Lindsey Wallace, Naomi Brady, and Aubry Nicholson: thank you for your particular love, and for being aunties to my children.

I am beyond grateful for the love and support of early readers, day walkers, and brainstormers: Lois Welch, Nancy Cook, Jo-Ann Mapson, Sherry Simpson, Daniel T. Kline, Kim Rich, Josh Bower, Adel Alghamdi, Megan Kruse, Nick Meyers, Sean McCarrey, Michael Cooper, Darcey Fairchild, Carol McKinney, and Sarah Buzard. And to John Wilson and Randy Warner: you'll never see this work, but your contributions are felt still. Rest in peace, my friends. The many hilarious and good humans who make up the comedy community in Missoula have been a gift to my life, as have my bandmates through the years: Jed Nussbaum, David Wilbert, Clare Menahan, Ethan Ryan, and Jean Larmon, PhD. And to my Banjo Pants crew, who came into my life mere days after my father left it: Kjerstin Gurda, Adam Lohrmann, Bri Ewert, Zach Johnson, Alex and Peter Carr, Micah Sewell, and Zachary Carlsen. Thank you for holding me.

Three strong women were instrumental in dragging this book out of my heart and onto the page. I am indebted to Judy Blunt for encouraging me to write it. To Kelly Sundberg, PhD, for the 3 a.m. sounding board sessions. And to M. Jackson, PhD, for the final push.

Three more strong women at Green Writers Press took it up from there. My publisher, Dede Cummings, with her energy and drive. And my editors, Ferne Johansson and Rose Alexandre-Leach, with their kind, far-seeing, generous eyes, who worked magic on these pages. Women who lift other women up are our hope for the future.

I never planned on having a husband, but now that I do, I never plan on not having him. Thank you, Peet, for giving me somewhere to finally drop anchor. You're going to need to learn an instrument, though, to make this a real family band. And to my children, Isadora and Malcolm, I am so thankful I get to be your mom, and that I get to cheer you on as your futures unfold. When it comes time to tell your own stories you don't need my permission. But you have it, if you want it.